# KALI and Her YOGINIS

## Embracing the Divine Feminine

OCCULTIST - DAEMONOLATOR - ALCHEMIST

**BLUEROSE PUBLISHERS**
India | U.K.

Copyright © Meenakshii 2024

All rights reserved by author. No part of this publication may be reproduced, stored in a retrieval system or transmitted in any form or by any means, electronic, mechanical, photocopying, recording or otherwise, without the prior permission of the author. Although every precaution has been taken to verify the accuracy of the information contained herein, the publisher assumes no responsibility for any errors or omissions. No liability is assumed for damages that may result from the use of information contained within.

BlueRose Publishers takes no responsibility for any damages, losses, or liabilities that may arise from the use or misuse of the information, products, or services provided in this publication.

For permissions requests or inquiries regarding this publication,
please contact:

BLUEROSE PUBLISHERS
www.BlueRoseONE.com
info@bluerosepublishers.com
+91 8882 898 898
+4407342408967

ISBN: 978-93-5819-305-3

Cover design: Meenakshii
Typesetting: Rohit

First Edition: January 2024

Email: creativity.magick@gmail.com
Website: www.magickinblack.com
Instagram: FolkloreMagick

*"In the myriad dance of life, Kali is my all -
my Guru, guiding with profound wisdom;
my friend, sharing in my deepest joys and sorrows;
my lover, embracing my soul in its rawest form;
my sister, walking beside me with empathy and strength;
my mother, nurturing my spiritual essence.
In her, I find the universe; she is the essence
and entirety of my existence."*

# The Divine Dance

In the realm where time and eternity embrace, Kali and Shiva, in a cosmic grace. Destroyers, regenerators, in their celestial flight, In their dance, the universe finds its light.

Beneath the starlit canopy, where dreams take flight, Lakshmi and Vishnu, in nurturing delight. Preservers of life, in an eternal embrace, In their love, the world finds its grace.

And where wisdom's rivers flow deep and wide, Saraswati and Brahma, side by side. Creators, thinkers, in their realm so vast, In their knowledge, the seeds of future are cast.

In these divine dances, where shadows meet light, Unfolds the universe, in its majestic might. In their embrace, the cosmic tales spun, The dance of creation, never undone.

So, we begin, with hearts open and eyes wide, Guided by divinity, in whom we confide. In their footsteps, our journey takes flight, A quest for the eternal, in the spiritual night.

*To all the guiding spirits, whose influence has shaped me into who I am today, I extend my deepest gratitude and love. Your unseen presence has been a cornerstone of my journey.*

*To my cherished followers, clients, and students: you have been my teachers in countless ways. Your presence in my life has been instrumental in my growth. Without you, I would not have reached the heights I have today. Your challenges and support have been invaluable lessons in my path.*

*To my ancestors, whose legacy flows through my veins, I offer my love and respect. Your stories, struggles, and triumphs live on within me.*

*To the daemonic forces that lifted me from my falls, I owe a debt of gratitude. Your tough love has been a catalyst for my resilience and strength.*

*To my magnificent mother, the dark queen of the night, thank you for the trials you've put me through. In the darkest of times, it was your guidance that I chose above all else, shaping me into a stronger, more dedicated individual.*

*To those who have loved me, your affection has been a source of joy and comfort. To those who have harboured negative feelings towards me, I thank you too. Your opposition has only fortified my resolve and helped mould me into who I am today.*

*To everyone who has hurt or blessed me, cursed or praised me, pushed or abandoned me, ignored or noticed me: each interaction has been a valuable piece of the mosaic that is my life.*

*A special acknowledgment goes to my team, whose unwavering support and dedication have been a pillar of our collective growth.*

*Finally, to the universe, I express my profound love and gratitude for this incredible life - a tapestry of adventure, learning, and growth.*

# Dedication:
# A Tribute to My Spiritual Lineage

As I pen these words, my heart overflows with a profound sense of gratitude and reverence. I find myself standing at the confluence of ancestral wisdom and divine grace, a privileged soul born into a family where spirituality is not just practiced but lived and breathed in every moment. This book, my humble offering to the cosmic dance of life, is a testament to the spiritual legacy I was born into, a legacy that has shaped my very being and my path.

My journey into the depths of spirituality began under the watchful eyes of my maternal grandparents, Late Sri Bijoy Ranjan Das and Late Smt. Sovana Das. Their devotion to Kali was not merely a practice; it was a way of life, an eternal flame that has been passed down through generations. Their unwavering faith, their daily rituals, and their embodiment of devotion carved the first steps of my spiritual path. They served with a love so profound that it transcended the bounds of the physical world, creating a sanctified space where I, too, could connect with the divine.

Equally influential in my spiritual upbringing was my paternal grandmother, Late Smt. Kalyani Guha. She was a beacon of light, guiding me through the potent world of Mantras. At the tender age of four, she introduced me to the profound observance of Maha Shiv Ratri, instilling in me a discipline and devotion that would become *the cornerstone of my life. Her hands gently guided mine as I learned to weave the sacred syllables of Devi Mantras, each chant a step deeper into the realm of the divine.*

*To be born into such a family is a blessing of immeasurable value. It is a privilege that has afforded me a unique perspective on life, an innate connection to the spiritual world, and a deep understanding of the sacred practices that form the bedrock of our existence. My grandparents, with their wisdom and their unwavering commitment to the divine path, were not just family; they were my first gurus, my spiritual north stars.*

*Their physical absence in this world leaves a void that is both poignant and profound. Yet, I know, as I embark on this journey of sharing my knowledge and experiences, that their spirits are with me, their blessings a guiding light. How I wish they could witness this endeavour, see how their teachings have blossomed into this work of heart and soul. I can almost hear their words of encouragement, feel their pride, and sense their joy.*

*As I stand at this juncture, ready to share my journey with you, dear reader, I offer my deepest gratitude. To my revered ancestors, for laying the foundation of my spiritual path; to the Supreme, for choosing me to walk this path and serve them; and to you, for joining me in this exploration of the divine. This book is more than a collection of words; it is a celebration of a legacy, a sharing of sacred wisdom, and an invitation to join me in the eternal dance of spirituality.*

*Let us embark on this journey together, with open hearts and inquisitive minds, as we explore the mysteries and the magnificence of the spiritual realm. May the blessings of my ancestors and the grace of the divine guide us on this path.*

*With heartfelt reverence and eternal gratitude...*

# A Gratitude-Filled Ode to My Mentors

*As I pause to reflect on the labyrinthine path that has been my spiritual journey, my heart swells with immense gratitude for the mentors who have graced my life. Like guiding stars in the vast cosmos, each one appeared at the precise moment I needed to ascend to the next echelon of understanding and consciousness. Their timely presence in my life's narrative is nothing short of miraculous, a testament to the universe's mysterious ways.*

*In every chapter of my spiritual quest, as I stood at the threshold of growth, a mentor emerged, holding the lantern of wisdom to light my way. It seemed as if the universe conspired to bring these enlightened souls into my life, each one arriving with a lesson I needed to learn, a truth I was ready to embrace. This beautiful synchronicity of guidance has been the backbone of my journey, carrying me across the tumultuous seas of doubt and uncertainty.*

*Each mentor has been a bridge, connecting me to higher realms of knowledge and experience. With their wisdom, they opened doors I didn't even know existed, guiding me through realms of esoteric knowledge, through intricate dances of spiritual practices. They were the hands that pulled me up when the climb was steep, the voices that whispered encouragement when the silence was overwhelming.*

*What I cherish most about my mentors is their selfless sharing of knowledge and experience. In their presence, I learned not just the tenets of spirituality but the art of being a mentor myself. Their examples have shown me that true wisdom is not just in knowing but in sharing, not just in leading but in nurturing.*

*Together, my mentors have woven a tapestry of collective wisdom in my soul. Their teachings, diverse yet harmonious, have shaped my understanding of the universe and my place within it. They have been the catalysts for transformations that I could scarcely have achieved alone.*

*As I extend my deepest gratitude to these remarkable individuals, I make a silent promise to honour their teachings by embodying them in my life and, in turn, being a guiding light to others. The journey of learning never ends, and as I continue on my path, I carry with me the invaluable gifts of their wisdom, love, and guidance.*

*To all my mentors, past, present, and future, I offer you my heartfelt thanks. You have not just taught me; you have enriched my being in ways words can scarcely capture. May I honour your contributions by becoming a beacon of wisdom, just as you have been for me.*

*With deepest gratitude and enduring reverence....*

# Preface

### *Kali and Her Yoginis -*
### *A Journey into Divine Transformation*

#### *A Tapestry of Spirituality and Empowerment*

Welcome, dear reader, to a journey that traverses the realms of the ancient and the mystical, a journey into the heart of divine transformation. "Kali and Her Yoginis" is more than a book; it is a spiritual odyssey that seeks to unravel the profound mysteries of one of the most enigmatic and powerful deities in the Hindu pantheon – My favourite –'Kali' & Her 'Yoginis'. This book is an invitation to explore the depths of Tantra, Kundalini, and the concept of free will within the context of spiritual growth and personal empowerment.

#### *The Essence of Kali and Her Yoginis*

At the heart of this book lies Kali, the Dark Mother, a symbol of strength, transformation, and the raw power of nature. This book aims to demystify Kali, presenting her not just as a figure of awe and reverence but as a metaphor for the transformative power within us all. It delves into her associations with Kundalini energy, exploring how these two potent forces are interwoven and reflective of each other.

Alongside her are Her Yoginis, each embodying a unique aspect of the divine feminine. Together, they represent a spectrum of energies that are crucial for understanding the dynamics of life, death, and rebirth.

### *A Guide for the Modern Seeker*

"Kali and Her Yoginis" is designed to resonate with the modern spiritual seeker. It bridges the gap between ancient teachings and contemporary spiritual practice, offering insights into how these timeless principles can be applied in today's world. From understanding the role of free will in spirituality to exploring different Tantra sects, this book provides a comprehensive guide for anyone looking to deepen their spiritual journey.

### *Tantra: Beyond Misconceptions*

In the chapters that unfold, the book addresses the often misunderstood concept of Tantra. Moving beyond the narrow association of Tantra with sexuality, we explore its diverse sects and practices, revealing Tantra as a comprehensive spiritual path that encompasses a wide spectrum of practices aimed at integrating all aspects of life into a higher consciousness.

### *The Role of Free Will in Spirituality*

A key theme of this book is the exploration of free will in the context of spirituality. We examine how the choices we make on our spiritual paths shape our destinies and how the path of Tantra, in particular, offers a unique perspective on the interplay between predestined life events and personal choices.

### For the Seeker of Spiritual Wisdom

A book designed for anyone who seeks a deeper understanding of the spiritual dimensions of existence. Whether you are a seasoned practitioner or a curious explorer, "Kali and Her Yoginis" offers insights into the transformative powers of the divine feminine and the universal energies that pervade our lives.

### A Guide to Personal and Universal Transformation

As you turn these pages, may you find the wisdom and inspiration to explore the depths of your own spirit. Each chapter is crafted to guide you through the nuances of Kali's symbolism, the empowering practices of Tantra, and the awakening of Kundalini energy. This journey is about understanding the cosmic interplay of energies and realizing the potential for personal and universal transformation.

### Embracing the Divine Dance

"Kali and Her Yoginis" is a homage to the divine dance of creation, preservation, and destruction. It is an exploration of how we, as part of this cosmic dance, can harness our inner energies to lead more empowered, aware, and fulfilling lives. May this book serve as a beacon on your path to spiritual discovery and enlightenment.

*Welcome to the journey. Let the dance begin.*
*Meenakshii*

# Where it all started...

At the tender age of sixteen, when dreams are vibrant and the heart is open to the mysteries of the universe, I found myself embarking on an unexpected spiritual odyssey. It began one fateful evening, as I wandered along a desolate path, shrouded in the twilight's embrace. There, emerging from the shadows stood a figure both awe-inspiring and unsettling – KALI, in all her fearsome glory.

Before me lay a ladder, its presence as incongruous as it was symbolic, leaning against the towering form of Kali. With a heart-pounding with both trepidation and intrigue, I began to ascend. Each rung brought me closer to Her, each step deepening my journey into the unknown.

As I neared Her, the surreal nature of the encounter intensified. In a twist of cosmic revelation, Kali transformed into Chinnamasta – the self-decapitated goddess, embodying the cycle of life, death, and rebirth. With a swift, decisive motion, she severed her own head with the Khadgam, a sacred sword symbolizing the cutting through of ignorance and ego.

As her golden head, radiant and formidable, descended from its celestial abode, time seemed to stand still. In an act of divine orchestration, it fell gently into my outstretched hands. The weight of it was not just physical but laden with the gravity of spiritual awakening.

Her eyes, those windows to cosmic wisdom, locked onto mine in an unbroken gaze. It was as if the very essence of the universe was peering into the depths of my soul, unveiling truths hidden in plain sight. The eyes of Chinnamasta, unflinching and penetrating, conveyed messages beyond the realm of spoken language, imparting wisdom that words could scarcely encapsulate.

This moment crystallized the paradox of life and death, creation and destruction that Chinnamasta so powerfully represents. The act of self-decapitation, far from being a morbid end, was a symbol of the continuous cycle of existence.

In the gaze of Chinnamasta, I felt a transformative realization wash over me. It was a stark reminder of the impermanence of life and the illusion of self. Yet, within this seemingly violent act, there lay a profound message of renewal and hope – a reminder that true liberation comes from within, often through the surrender of our deepest fears and attachments.

As the encounter reached its zenith, I understood that this vision was not a mere figment of imagination but a spiritual transmission of the highest order. Chinnamasta's severed head, cradled in my hands, became a sacred emblem of my journey henceforth – a journey of embracing life's mysteries, transcending the ego, and pursuing a path of enlightened understanding. In Her unyielding gaze, I found the courage to face the complexities of existence and the inspiration to seek a deeper, more profound understanding of the divine dance of creation.

This encounter, as abrupt in its end as in its beginning, marked my awakening from a deep slumber. At the young age of sixteen, I experienced my first communion with Chinnamasta, an initiation into a world of profound spiritual significance that I had scarcely imagined. This vivid experience became the genesis of a path I was destined to walk - a path illuminated by the enigmatic teachings of Chinnamasta. Her symbolism, complex and multi-layered, began to unravel before me, guiding me towards an understanding that transcended conventional wisdom.

As I journeyed deeper, Chinnamasta revealed her manifold nature – each aspect challenging my perceptions, each revelation beckoning me towards a deeper contemplation of life's paradoxes. She stood as a symbol of both the terrifying and the sublime, a deity who embodied the raw truth of existence in all its forms.

Thus, my life became intertwined with the teachings of Chinnamasta. Her presence, though initially daunting, unfolded as a source of immense wisdom and strength. Through her guidance, I learned to embrace life's complexities with grace, to see beyond the surface of things, and to find harmony in the dance of creation and destruction. In her, I found not just a goddess to revere but a teacher, a guide, and a beacon of enlightenment on my spiritual journey.

# My second Encounter –

**Whispers of the Veil: My Dance with Dhumavati**

Amid a life seeking spiritual depth, a profound encounter beckoned me, one that would forever alter my understanding of the divine feminine. It was on an evening, like any other, that the paths of destiny led me to a rendezvous with the mystical. As I walked the crowded streets, weaving through the cacophony of the mundane, my attention was inexplicably drawn to an elderly lady, cloaked in white, sitting alone on the steps of an overhead bridge. Her presence, an oasis of calm in the urban tumult, stirred something deep within me.

Compelled by an unseen force, I found myself turning back, drawn to offer assistance. There was an air of otherworldliness about her, her refined demeanour juxtaposed starkly against the grimy backdrop. As I approached her, a wave of inexplicable familiarity washed over me. It was as if this encounter was not by chance, but a moment written in the stars.

In the blink of an eye, the lady stood before me, her eyes – deep and dark as the night sky – locking onto mine. A touch, gentle yet electrifying, upon my wrist, and the world as I knew it dissolved. Suddenly, I was transported to an expanse of desert, an endless horizon where the universe unfolded before me. The

'Brahmand' lay open, a cosmic canvas of creation and dissolution.

Snapped back to the bustling street, the surreal experience lingered like a dream at dawn. I asked her, "How may I assist you?" Her voice, tinged with the weight of aeons, spoke of a need to return home to her 'Gopal', yet hindered by a shortage of mere 350 rupees. Without hesitation, I handed her all the money I possessed – a small price for a glimpse into the infinite.

As quickly as she appeared, she vanished, leaving behind a trail of mystery. My colleague and I, our minds entwined in bewilderment, sought answers from passers-by, but it was as if she had never existed to anyone but us.

It was not until later, amidst my studies of Kali, that an aged teacher illuminated my mind with a revelation – the mysterious lady was Dhumavati herself. Unlike many whose journey with the divine feminine begins with Kali or Tara, mine was initiated by Chinnamasta and Dhumavati, hinting at a spiritual quest transcending lifetimes.

Dhumavati, the 'smoky one', emerged as a symbol of the impermanent, the decaying. Her form – an old, haggard woman crowned with skulls and astride crows – is often misconstrued as malevolent. Yet, within her lies a wellspring of wisdom. She embodies the ephemeral nature of existence, teaching lessons of detachment, acceptance, and the finding of peace amidst life's tumultuous dance.

Through Dhumavati, I learned to navigate the shadows of life, finding light in the darkness, strength in vulnerability, and wisdom amidst ignorance. Her teachings, though shrouded in mystery, reveal the path to inner peace and liberation – a journey of letting go and embracing the cosmic dance of existence.

My encounter with Dhumavati was not merely an encounter with a deity but a dance with the divine feminine itself. In her, I found a guide who led me through the complexities of life, teaching me to embrace the transient nature of the world and to find harmony within. As I continue on my spiritual path, her teachings remain a beacon, guiding me towards a deeper understanding of the universe and my place within it. In the dance with Dhumavati, I find the rhythm of my soul, moving gracefully towards enlightenment and eternal peace.

# Contents

*The Divine Dance* ............................................................. v
*Dedication: A Tribute to My Spiritual Lineage* ..................... vii
*A Gratitude-Filled Ode to My Mentors* ............................... ix
*Preface* ............................................................................. xi
*Where it all started...* ...................................................... xiv
*My second Encounter –* .................................................. xvii

1. Ganesha: The Beloved Son of Aadi Shakti ..................... 3
2. Prelude: The Call to Divine Guidance ............................ 9
3. Understanding the Fear Surrounding Kali: Beyond Misconceptions ............................................................ 13
4. The Interplay of Free Will and Spirituality: The Path of Conscious Choice ...................................................... 19
5. Harmonizing the Eternal: The Convergence of Physics and Spirituality ........................................................... 31
6. Awakening the Serpent Power: The Transformational Journey of Kundalini .................................................. 35
7. Harnessing the Power of Kali and Her Yoginis: Transforming Energy, Transforming Lives .................... 40
8. Kali and Her Yoginis: Unleashing the Power Within .... 43

9. The Dance of Eternity: Kali and Mahakaal................... 49
10. Kali Sahasranama....................................................... 63
11. Mahavidhyas............................................................ 115
12. The Yoginis :........................................................... 161
13. The Mystique of Kama Kala: Exploring the
    Esoteric Realms....................................................... 207
14. The Luminous Paths of Chandra Kala and Surya Kala .. 212
15. The Dance of Karma: Destiny, Time, and the
    Spiritual Path.......................................................... 221

*Acknowledgements: Temples of Transformation* ................... *231*

*Chapter : 1*

# Ganesha:
# The Beloved Son of Aadi Shakti

At the heart of our spiritual journey into Tantra stands Lord Ganesha, revered as 'Aadi Shakti's Priya Putra' – the beloved son of the Primeval Energy, Aadi Shakti. This profound connection between Ganesha and Aadi Shakti is not just of maternal lineage but also deeply symbolic, representing the intricate relationship between the primal forces of existence and our own spiritual journey.

Legend narrates the unique birth of Ganesha, emerging from the skin impurities of Aadi Shakti. This origin story is symbolic, representing how even the most basic elements can give rise to divine manifestations. Ganesha, born out of such humble origins, becomes a deity intrinsically linked to the earth and its grounding energies.

This connection with the earth aligns Ganesha with the Muladhara chakra, the root chakra located at the base of the spine. The Muladhara is where our basic instincts, survival needs, and primal urges reside. Ganesha's association with this chakra makes him a pivotal deity in addressing our fundamental human experiences and instincts.

As the deity who presides over beginnings and thresholds, Ganesha's link to the Muladhara also extends to our basic urges and desires (Kama). He is seen as the guide who helps navigate these primal energies, not to suppress them but to understand and channel them in a way that supports spiritual growth.

### *He is The Gateway to Higher Consciousness*

Ganesha's role as the son of Aadi Shakti (Parvati) and his connection to the Muladhara chakra make him a crucial figure in Tantric practices. He is always invoked at the start of any spiritual endeavour as the one who lays the foundation for the ascent to higher consciousness. By harmonizing our basic instincts and grounding energies, Ganesha paves the way for Kundalini Shakti's upward journey through the chakras.

In Tantric traditions, where the journey of spiritual awakening is as much about embracing the material as transcending it, Ganesha's role becomes paramount. As we commence our exploration of Tantra under his guidance, we recognize Ganesha as the deity who grounds us, aligns our basic energies, and opens the path to higher spiritual realms. He is the initial key to unlocking the vast potential within, guiding us from the realm of the Muladhara to the heights of spiritual enlightenment and that is why we would start this journey with His prayers and the explanation as perceived by me.

*Prayer to Lord Ganesha*

Om Ganaanaam tvaa
Ganapatigum Havaamahe Kavim Kavinaam
Upamasravas tamam
Jyestha Raajam Brahmanaam
Brahmanaspata Aa nah Srinvan
Ootibhih Seeda Saadanam
Sri Maha Ganapataye Namah

*Invoking the Pathfinder - Lord Ganesha and the Journey of Tantra*

At the threshold of our spiritual journey into the depths of Tantra, we commence with an invocation to Ganesha. He is not just a deity but a symbol of auspicious beginnings, the harbinger of wisdom, and the remover of obstacles. As we embark on this profound path, it is under His benevolent guidance that we seek to explore the mystical realms of Tantra.

*The Gateway to Spiritual Wisdom*

Lord Ganesha, with his elephantine countenance and gentle, yet powerful demeanour, stands as the sentinel at the gates of spiritual awakening. In the pantheon of Hindu deities, he is the 'Vighnaharta' – the one who dispels all hurdles, and the 'Buddhi Pradayaka' – the giver of wisdom. His presence at the onset of this journey symbolizes the unlocking of deeper esoteric truths, the kindling of insightful understanding necessary for the exploration of Tantra.

*Invocation of the Divine*

Our journey begins with the sacred verse, "Om Ganaanaam tvaa / Ganapatigum Havaamahe." This chant is more than mere words; it is an invocation that sets the spiritual stage, inviting Ganesha's guiding presence into our quest. The term "Gana" signifies the collective – a myriad of elements that constitute our existence, and He is revered as their master, orchestrating the cosmic dance with a wisdom that transcends the ordinary.

### *Offering of the Self: A Symbolic Act*

As we chant and offer ghee into the sacred fire, we engage in an act of spiritual surrender. This ritual symbolizes the pouring of our innermost fears, anxieties, and limitations – often rooted in the Muladhara chakra – into the divine flame. It is a gesture of releasing those barriers that impede our spiritual ascent, entrusting them to the transformative power of Ganesha.

### *The Poet's Heart: A Metaphor for Transcendence*

In seeking Ganesha's blessings, we aspire to rise to the state of a 'Kavi' – a poet. This metaphor extends beyond the literal sense, embodying a seeker who can articulate the profound, the sublime, and the essence that lies beyond the grasp of mere intellect. The poet here is an enlightened soul who perceives the truth in its purest form, uncoloured by biases, seeing the world with dispassionate clarity and a balanced sense of humour.

Revered as "jyestharaja," the foremost among gods, Lord Ganesha's role transcends removing physical obstacles; he is the divine orchestrator who guides us through internal challenges, fostering growth and enlightenment. His guidance teaches us to navigate life's twists with a sense of humour and light-heartedness, finding joy even amidst trials.

As we invoke Lord Ganesha, our plea – "Aa nah Srinvan / Ootibhih Seeda Saadanam" – is an earnest call for his attention and grace. We seek a path that is harmonious, uncluttered by complexities, a journey where every step is an evolution towards spiritual fulfilment.

Thus, our invocation to Lord Ganesha is not just the beginning of a book or a journey; it is an initiation into a transformative process. It is a commitment to walk the path of Tantra under the watchful, compassionate gaze of the Divine Pathfinder. As we surrender our limitations and embrace the wisdom he bestows, we embark on a journey of profound self-discovery and spiritual liberation, guided by the gentle yet powerful Lord Ganesha.

In the resplendent universe Ganesha commands a special place as the 'चौसष्ट कलांचा अधिपती' - the master of the 64 arts. This title not only signifies his expertise across a vast array of disciplines but also symbolizes his profound embodiment of wisdom and knowledge. As we delve into the myriad arts mastered by Lord Ganesha, we come to understand why he is revered as the supreme teacher and guide in our spiritual and worldly endeavours.

### *The Diverse Spectrum of the 64 Arts (Kala)*

Lord Ganesha's mastery of the 64 arts presents a kaleidoscope of skills that encompass both the sacred and the secular, ranging from the arts of music and dance to the sciences of engineering and medicine. Each art form, a reflection of Ganesha's multifaceted nature, offers insights into the depths of his wisdom.

*Chapter : 2*

# Prelude: The Call to Divine Guidance

As we embark on this profound journey, it's essential to pause and contemplate on a pivotal question: Who truly needs the guidance of Kali and Her Yoginis? In the spiritual realm, where paths intersect and diverge in myriad ways, understanding the calling of one's heart and soul is crucial. The path of Kali and Her Yoginis, rich in depth and intensity, beckons not just anyone, but those who resonate with certain spiritual needs and aspirations.

Kali, the Dark Mother, embodies transformation, strength, and the fierce aspect of divine love. Her Yoginis, each a manifestation of divine energies, offer a spectrum of spiritual insights and experiences. Their guidance is a beacon for those traversing the labyrinth of spiritual growth, seeking not just enlightenment but a profound metamorphosis of the self.

In the following discourse, we delve into the archetypes of seekers for whom the path of Kali and Her Yoginis is most suited. This exploration is not just about identifying who these individuals might be, but also about understanding the nature of the spiritual quest they embark upon – a quest that is as challenging as it is rewarding, as demanding as it is liberating.

As we prepare to uncover who stands to gain the most from their guidance, let us open our minds and hearts to the transformative power of Kali and Her Yoginis. Their path is one of radical self-acceptance, fierce grace, and the transcendence of conventional boundaries. It is a journey for those who dare to embrace the depths of their being, confront their shadows, and emerge empowered and enlightened.

### *Who needs the guidance of Kali and Her Yoginis?*

The guidance of Kali and Her Yoginis is particularly resonant for individuals who are seeking empowerment. These powerful deities symbolize aspects of the divine feminine that are profound and transformative, making their guidance suitable for those on a path of significant personal and spiritual growth. Here are some key characteristics of individuals who might seek the guidance of Kali and Her Yoginis:

***Seekers of Spiritual Depth:*** Those who are not satisfied with superficial understandings of spirituality and are seeking a deeper, more experiential engagement with the divine.

***Individuals Facing Major Life Transitions:*** Kali's energy is particularly relevant for those undergoing significant life changes or transitions, as she symbolizes the destruction of the old and the birth of the new.

***Practitioners of Tantra:*** Given Kali's central role in Tantric practices, those who are drawn to or currently practicing Tantra may seek her guidance to deepen their spiritual journey.

***Confronting Personal Darkness:*** Individuals facing their inner shadows, fears, or any form of psychological and emotional turmoil may find refuge and strength in Kali's transformative power.

***Feminine Empowerment Seekers:*** Women, and also men, seeking to connect with or enhance the feminine aspects of their spirituality may be drawn to Kali and Her Yoginis for empowerment and inspiration.

***Practitioners Seeking Liberation:*** Kali's aspect as a liberator from illusion and ego makes her guidance sought after by those who are on a path to moksha, or liberation.

***Healers and Spiritual Guides:*** Those who are in healing or guiding professions may seek Kali's wisdom to enhance their ability to help others through transformative processes.

***Artists and Creatives:*** Individuals in creative fields may be drawn to the dynamic and transformative energy of Kali and Her Yoginis to fuel their creative expression.

***Yoga Practitioners and Meditators:*** Those engaged in advanced yoga practices and meditation might find the energy of Kali and Her Yoginis conducive to deepening their practice.

***Devotees of the Goddess Tradition:*** Followers of the Goddess tradition in various cultures might resonate with Kali's symbolism and seek her guidance as part of their broader spiritual practice.

It is important to approach the worship or guidance of Kali and Her Yoginis with respect, understanding, and a sincere heart. Given the powerful nature of these deities, guidance from a knowledgeable teacher, guru, or guide is highly recommended, especially for those new to these practices. This ensures a safe, respectful, and fruitful engagement with these profound aspects of the divine feminine.

## Chapter : 3

# Understanding the Fear Surrounding Kali: Beyond Misconceptions

*The Formidable Image of Kali*

Kali's portrayal is undeniably formidable: a dark complexion, a garland of human skulls, a skirt of severed arms, her tongue lolling out in a battle cry, and her foot dominantly on Lord Shiva's chest. This depiction, rich in symbolism, can be stark and unnerving. In the traditional lore, Kali is the destroyer of demons, a symbol of cosmic justice. Her fierceness, often misinterpreted, is the first layer of fear associated with her.

The fear of Kali partly arises from cultural contexts that often equate darkness with negativity. Kali's dark form is mistakenly aligned with malevolence, overlooking her role as a fierce protector against evil. In cultures that favour demure and gentle depictions of the divine, Kali's aggressive posture is seen as an anomaly, furthering the fear surrounding her.

Kali embodies the cycle of creation, sustenance, and destruction – essential to Hindu cosmology. Her destructive aspect, symbolizing the end of cycles, aligns with concepts of death and endings, which are inherently feared in human psychology. The dread of destruction and the unknown it represents contributes significantly to the fear associated with Kali.

In the intricate web of spiritual traditions, Kali stands as the prime deity of Tantra, a path often shrouded in mystery and misinterpretation. This association with Tantra, particularly its misunderstood aspects, contributes significantly to the fear surrounding Kali. Tantra, in its essence, is a profound spiritual practice that aims at the liberation and expansion of consciousness through various rituals and meditative techniques. However, in popular culture, Tantra has often been mistakenly linked with black magic, leading to a widespread misconception of its true purpose. This misalignment with the darker, more sensational aspects of esoteric practices has cast a shadow over Kali's image, painting her as a deity to be feared rather than revered. Her portrayal as a powerful, fierce goddess in Tantric practices only adds to this aura of apprehension. The fear, therefore, stems not just from her formidable depiction but also from a lack of understanding of Tantra's deeper spiritual significance and its role in harnessing the divine energy within us. This misunderstanding underscores the need for a deeper exploration and education about the true nature of Tantra and Kali's place within it, as symbols of transformation, liberation, and the ultimate union with the divine.

Kali demands a confrontation with the inner self, a journey that can be turbulent and intense. This transformative aspect involves the dissolution of ego and falsehoods, a process that can be daunting. The fear of what this deep introspection and change might unveil in one's self is a powerful reason many hesitate to embrace Kali's influence fully.

Kali's 'Wrath' – A common fear is that improper reverence of Kali might invoke her wrath. This fear stems from a misunderstanding of Kali's nature. In Hinduism, deities' actions are often viewed as reflections of one's karma rather than arbitrary punishment. Kali's 'backlash' is more about the natural consequences of actions and the intense nature of spiritual growth.

The history of Kali worship, particularly in certain periods and among various groups, has contributed significantly to the fear and misunderstandings surrounding her. Indeed, there have been instances, especially in the past, where Kali was worshipped by dacoits (bandits) and other fringe groups who, misguided in their interpretations, performed extreme rituals including, allegedly, human sacrifices. Such practices were never a part of mainstream Hinduism or Tantra but were the result of distorted beliefs held by these outlawed factions.

This dark chapter in Kali worship has left an indelible mark on her perception. Even today, sporadic reports of illicit groups engaging in similar practices in the name of Kali or Tantra further exacerbate the fear and misunderstanding. These actions, often sensationalized by the media and popular culture, have unfortunately contributed to a skewed perception of Kali as a bloodthirsty deity and Tantra as a path of dark magic.

It is essential to understand that these practices are in stark contrast to the authentic teachings and traditions of Tantra and Kali worship. In its true form, Tantra is a complex spiritual path focusing on inner transformation and the realization of one's divine nature. Similarly, Kali, in the broader Hindu spiritual context, is revered as a powerful symbol of time, change, and liberation, far removed from the negative associations of violence and fear.

The misdeeds of a few who have misused Kali's name and the tenets of Tantra for unrighteous practices should not overshadow the profound spiritual significance these hold. It is important to differentiate between these aberrations and the true, rich spiritual heritage they represent. In essence, Kali's worship and Tantra require understanding, respect, and a deep commitment to spiritual ethics, guiding practitioners towards enlightenment and inner peace, not fear and darkness.

In modern spiritual discourses, there is an evolving understanding of Kali, focusing on her aspects as an emblem of empowerment, liberation, and the raw power of nature. This contemporary interpretation encourages a re-evaluation of the fear associated with her, advocating a view of Kali as a guide through life's transformative challenges.

Understanding Kali requires going beyond superficial interpretations and delving into the deeper symbolism of her nature. To fully grasp the essence of Kali requires peeling back layers of cultural, historical, and psychological interpretations, venturing into the deep symbolism of her nature. Recognizing the fear associated with her as a reflection of our internal struggles and resistance to change is crucial. Embracing Kali in her entirety invites a journey of empowerment and profound transformation. This chapter challenges readers to transcend their fears and misconceptions, seeing Kali not merely as an object of terror but as a pivotal force of life's dynamic rhythm, guiding us through the endless cycles of existence.

## Chapter : 4

# The Interplay of Free Will and Spirituality: The Path of Conscious Choice

### *The Essence of Free Will in Spiritual Growth*

Free will is the gift of choice, the power to shape our destiny and carve our unique paths in the universe. This essay delves into the importance of free will in spirituality, examining how our conscious choices are fundamental to our spiritual growth and understanding.

### *The Concept of Free Will in Various Spiritual Traditions*

Different spiritual traditions view free will through various lenses. In many Eastern philosophies, free will is often interwoven with concepts like karma and dharma, suggesting a balance between personal choice and cosmic law. In Western theology, free will is frequently discussed in the context of moral responsibility and divine grace. Despite these differences, the common thread across cultures is the recognition of free will as a crucial aspect of the human experience.

Free will empower individuals to take charge of their spiritual journey. It is through conscious choices that we navigate the waters of life, learning from our experiences and growing in wisdom. The exercise of free will is not just about making choices but about understanding the consequences of those choices, both for ourselves and the world around us.

The debate between predestination and free will is longstanding. In spirituality, this interplay is often seen as a dance between the soul's destiny and the choices we make. While certain events in life might be preordained, how we respond to these events is where free will comes into play. This dynamic creates a space where personal growth and spiritual evolution can occur.

In exercising free will, there is also a moral dimension. Spiritual traditions often emphasize the need for ethical choices and living in harmony with universal laws. The decisions made through free will are seen as reflections of one's inner moral compass, shaping not only individual destiny but also contributing to the collective consciousness.

The path of free will is not without its challenges. It involves facing the consequences of our actions, which can be both rewarding and difficult. However, it is through these challenges that spiritual growth is catalyzed. Each decision, each crossroad faced, becomes an opportunity for deeper understanding and advancement on the spiritual path.

Free will is an integral part of the spiritual journey. It is through our choices that we define ourselves and our paths towards enlightenment. By embracing and responsibly exercising our free will, we open ourselves to a multitude of possibilities and opportunities for growth. It is a tool for transformation, a means to engage with the universe in a meaningful way, and a catalyst for becoming architects of our spiritual destiny.

## *The Freedom of Spiritual Choice: Embracing Tantra across Cultures*

At the core of human existence lies the profound power of choice, particularly evident in our spiritual endeavors. While many are born into specific religious traditions, the journey of spirituality transcends these initial boundaries. It is in this context that Tantra emerges as a universal path, accessible and adaptable across various cultural and religious backgrounds.

## *Beyond Birth Religion: The Universal Appeal of Tantra*

Tantra, often misunderstood and sometimes misrepresented, is in essence a holistic approach to spirituality. It is not confined to a single religious doctrine but is a spiritual science that transcends cultural and religious barriers. Anyone, irrespective of their birth religion, can explore and practice Tantra. This path emphasizes the unity of all aspects of life and consciousness, offering a comprehensive approach to spiritual development.

## *The Weave of Life and Spirit*

The word 'Tantra' itself means to weave or to expand. It represents a fabric of practices, philosophies, and rituals that integrate the physical, mental, and spiritual dimensions of life. Tantra sees the universe as a cosmic weave of the material and the spiritual, where every thread is interconnected.

## *Embracing the Divine Feminine: Devi Sadhana*

Within the realm of Tantra lies the profound practice of the Divine Feminine. This aspect of Tantra is not just about external worship but about recognizing and honouring the divine feminine energy within oneself. It is about connecting with and awakening the Shakti – the primordial cosmic energy – that resides within every individual.

Tantra is a path of liberation – a means to transcend the limitations imposed by societal norms and personal conditioning. It empowers practitioners to explore their spirituality in a way that is authentic and personal, breaking free from the constraints of orthodox religious practices. Through Tantra, practitioners learn to embrace their innate power and wisdom, leading to a deeper understanding and acceptance of themselves and the universe.

### *The Practices of Tantra*

Tantric practices are diverse, ranging from meditation, mantra chanting, and ritualistic worship, to more esoteric practices involving yoga, breathwork, and the channeling of energy. These practices are designed to harmonize the body, mind, and spirit, leading to a state of heightened awareness and spiritual unity.

Despite its openness and inclusivity, Tantra is grounded in strong ethical principles. It emphasizes the importance of intention, respect, and responsibility in all practices. The path of Tantra is not a pursuit of mere pleasure or power but a journey towards spiritual enlightenment and the harmonious balance of all life's forces.

The path of Tantra, with its emphasis on personal experience and spiritual freedom, resonates deeply with the concept of free will in spirituality. It represents a conscious choice to explore and embrace a holistic spiritual path, transcending religious boundaries. Through the practice of Tantra, and particularly through Devi Sadhana, individuals from any religious background can embark on a transformative journey, discovering the divine weave of life and the universe within themselves. This chapter encourages seekers to embrace the Tantric path as a profound expression of their spiritual freedom and a step towards universal harmony and enlightenment.

## *Demystifying Tantra: Beyond the Misconceptions: Misunderstood Tantra*

In the contemporary spiritual landscape, Tantra is often shrouded in misconception and controversy, largely due to its association with sexuality. This chapter aims to clarify these misunderstandings, highlighting Tantra's true essence as a path to divine union and elaborating on its various forms.

### *The Misconception of Tantra and Sexuality*

The most common misconception about Tantra is its reduction to merely a sexual practice. This skewed perception has been fuelled by popular culture and a superficial understanding of its teachings. While Tantra does not shy away from embracing sexuality as a part of the human experience, it is not its central focus. Tantra is about the integration and transformation of all aspects of life, including sexuality, into a higher spiritual consciousness.

At its core, Tantra is a spiritual path aimed at achieving a profound union with the divine. It is a holistic system that sees the divine in everything, teaching that spiritual enlightenment can be attained through the conscious experience and integration of all aspects of life, not just through asceticism or renunciation.

Tantra is a rich, multifaceted tradition that offers a path to spiritual liberation through the integration of all life experiences. It teaches that enlightenment can be found in the ordinary and that every aspect of human life, including sexuality, can be a gateway to the divine. By understanding the true nature of Tantra and its various forms, practitioners can embark on a holistic spiritual journey that respects and utilizes the full spectrum of human experience. Here we aim to align with the understanding of Tantra, moving beyond misconceptions to embrace its profound and transformative potential.

Often misunderstood in its essence and practices, it encompasses a wide spectrum of paths and teachings. Each sect of Tantra offers a unique approach to spiritual realization, reflecting the diversity and richness of this ancient tradition. This essay delves deeper into the various Tantra sects, providing clarity and insight into their distinct practices and philosophies.

### *The Diversity and Unity of Tantra*

The diverse sects of Tantra offer a rich array of paths for spiritual seekers, each with its unique practices and philosophical underpinnings. From the purity of White Tantra to the radical approaches of Left-Hand Tantra, this tradition provides a spectrum of options for individuals at different stages of their spiritual journey. Understanding these diverse paths allows practitioners to choose a Tantra sect that resonates with their personal inclinations and spiritual goals, highlighting Tantra's inclusive and transformative nature.

### *White Tantra (Shukla Tantra)*

White Tantra is often associated with purity and spiritual refinement. It focuses on practices that cultivate mental clarity, emotional balance, and spiritual awakening. Key elements include:

***Meditation and Visualization:*** Techniques aimed at expanding consciousness and achieving higher states of awareness.

***Mantra and Sound:*** Utilizing sacred sounds and vibrations for healing and spiritual elevation.

***Yogic Practices:*** Physical and breathing exercises designed to purify the body and mind.

*Subcategories of White Tantra (Shukla Tantra)*

White Tantra, focused on purification and spiritual elevation, branches into several practices:

***Raja Yoga Tantra:*** Emphasizes meditation and mental control to achieve self-realization.

***Bhakti Yoga Tantra:*** Focuses on devotional practices and loving surrender to the divine.

***Jnana Yoga Tantra:*** Involves the path of knowledge and wisdom to attain enlightenment.

White Tantra is generally considered the most accessible and widely practiced form, suitable for individuals seeking a path of gentle spiritual growth and self-development.

### Red Tantra (Rakta Tantra)

Red Tantra is perhaps the most misunderstood, often equated solely with sexual practices. However, its scope is broader, encompassing the transformation of all physical experiences into spiritual growth. Its practices include:

***Sacred Sexuality:*** Viewing sexual union as a powerful tool for spiritual connection and energy exchange.

***Physicality as a Path to Enlightenment:*** Embracing the body and physical experiences as integral to spiritual awakening.

***Energy Work:*** Harnessing and channelling sexual energy for healing and spiritual ascension.

Red Tantra is for those who wish to engage deeply with their physicality and use it as a means of spiritual connection and growth.

### Subcategories of Red Tantra (Rakta Tantra)

Red Tantra, known for its physical and energetic practices, includes:

***Kundalini Tantra:*** Focuses on awakening the Kundalini energy through yoga and meditation.

***Maithuna Tantra:*** Involves ritualistic sexual practices symbolizing the union of divine energies.

***Prana Tantra:*** Utilizes breath work to harness and channel life force energy.

### Black Tantra (Krishna Tantra)

Black Tantra is often associated with the use of occult practices and confronting darker aspects of the psyche. It is not inherently negative but rather focuses on:

***Shadow Work:*** Delving into and transforming the darker parts of the self.

***Occult Practices:*** Utilizing rituals, symbols, and mantras to work with unseen energies.

***Transmutation of Energies:*** Converting negative energies into positive, transformative forces.

*Subcategories of Black Tantra (Krishna Tantra)*

Black Tantra, dealing with the transformation of darker energies, comprises:

***Aghora Tantra:*** Engages with taboo practices to attain liberation and power.

***Kaula Tantra:*** Involves complex rituals and can include elements of Left-Hand practices.

***Nath Tantra:*** Focuses on mastery over physical and spiritual elements, often using secretive practices.

Black Tantra is usually recommended for advanced practitioners under the guidance of an experienced teacher due to its intense and complex nature.

*Yellow Tantra*

Yellow Tantra combines aspects of ritual, astrology, and alchemy. Its focus is on:

***Cosmic Alignment:*** Aligning individual energy with cosmic forces through astrological understanding.

***Alchemical Practices:*** Transforming the base aspects of the self into higher spiritual energies.

***Ritualistic Worship:*** Employing elaborate rituals to connect with divine energies.

### Subcategories of Yellow Tantra

Yellow Tantra, integrating elements of ritual and alchemy, includes:

***Siddha Tantra:*** Emphasizes achieving supernatural abilities or siddhis.

***Astrological Tantra:*** Involves aligning one's spiritual practice with astrological influences.

***Ritualistic Tantra:*** Utilizes detailed rituals as a pathway to spiritual attainment.

Yellow Tantra is often intertwined with traditional religious practices and requires a deep understanding of symbolic systems and rituals.

### Left-Hand Tantra (Vama Marga)

Left-Hand Tantra is known for its unconventional and often transgressive practices. It challenges societal norms to achieve spiritual liberation:

***Breaking Taboos:*** Engaging in practices that defy conventional social and moral norms.

***Direct Confrontation of Fears:*** Using what is typically forbidden or feared as a path to enlightenment.

***Non-Dualistic Approach:*** Embracing all aspects of life, both pure and impure, as part of the divine.

### Subcategories of Left-Hand Tantra (Vama Marga)

Left-Hand Tantra, known for its non-conventional approach, has variations like:

***Sahajiya Tantra:*** Emphasizes spontaneous and natural expression as a path to enlightenment.

***Veera Tantra:*** Focuses on overcoming internal and external obstacles through bold practices.

***Kapalika Tantra:*** Involves practices associated with cremation grounds and confronting death.

Left-Hand Tantra is suited for those who seek a path of radical self-acceptance and are willing to challenge deeply held beliefs and norms.

### Right-Hand Tantra (Dakshina Marga)

In contrast to Left-Hand Tantra, Right-Hand Tantra adheres to traditional societal and moral values. Its practices are more conservative, focusing on:

***Inner Purification:*** Emphasizing personal discipline, ethical behaviour, and mental purity.

***Conventional Rituals:*** Following traditional rituals and practices in a structured manner.

***Spiritual Discipline:*** Maintaining strict adherence to spiritual doctrines and teachings.

### Subcategories of Right-Hand Tantra (Dakshina Marga)

Right-Hand Tantra, with its more orthodox practices, includes:

***Vedanta Tantra:*** Integrates the philosophical teachings of the Vedanta with Tantric practices.

***Samaya Tantra:*** Involves internal, symbolic worship without the need for external rituals.

***Dakshinachara Tantra:*** Adheres to social norms and traditional ritualistic worship.

Right-Hand Tantra is suitable for individuals seeking a structured and disciplined path to spiritual growth within the boundaries of conventional norms.

The various subcategories within each Tantra sect reveal the depth and diversity of this spiritual path. From the meditative focus of Raja Yoga Tantra to the spontaneous expressions of Sahajiya Tantra, these sub-traditions offer a range of practices catering to different spiritual inclinations and goals. This chapter invites readers to explore the layered dimensions of Tantra, encouraging a deeper understanding of its rich and complex nature. As practitioners delve into these subcategories, they can find a Tantric path that resonates most profoundly with their personal journey towards spiritual fulfilment.

## Chapter : 5

# Harmonizing the Eternal: The Convergence of Physics and Spirituality

In the tapestry of human understanding, there exist two seemingly divergent threads: physics and spirituality. For centuries, these domains were perceived as distinct – one rooted in empirical investigation and the other in transcendent experience. Yet, as our grasp of the universe expands, we find these paths not diverging, but converging, revealing a profound interconnectedness that binds the physical and the metaphysical.

### *The Historical Perspective*

Historically, the mysteries of the universe were contemplated by sages and scientists alike. Ancient civilizations looked to deities and spirits to explain the unexplainable, weaving narratives that filled the gaps in human understanding. Spirituality was not just a belief system but a lens through which the early humans made sense of their world – a precursor to what we now call science.

### *The Laws of Nature and Metaphysics*

In the realm of fundamental physics, laws such as gravity, electromagnetism, and quantum mechanics describe the machinations of the universe. These laws, precise and predictable, are the language of science. Parallel to this, spirituality speaks of metaphysical laws – principles governing the unseen, the energies and vibrations that connect all life. Here, the concept of 'spirit' in metaphysics finds its counterpart in the 'energy' studied by science.

### *Energy: The Common Thread*

Energy is a concept that beautifully bridges physics and spirituality. In physics, it is the capacity to perform work, to cause change – it is omnipresent, neither created nor destroyed. Spiritually, energy is the essence of life and consciousness, a force that animates and connects. This parallel draws a compelling line between the seen and the unseen, the tangible and the intangible.

### *Quantum Physics: The Meeting Point*

Quantum physics, with its exploration of the subatomic realm, has further blurred the line between these two worlds. Concepts like entanglement and superposition resonate with spiritual ideas of interconnectedness and the coexistence of multiple states of being. It suggests a universe more intricate and interconnected than we ever imagined, one where consciousness might play a fundamental role.

### *Practical Implications*

This convergence has practical implications. Understanding the interconnectedness of all things can lead to a more holistic approach to life, one that honours both the physical and the spiritual. It can influence how we approach healing, creativity, transformation marked by the destruction of old patterns and the creation of new paths.

Understanding the unity of Kali and Kundalini energies is key to harnessing this transformative power. It involves recognizing that the fierce, liberating energy of Kali is not external but lies within, embodied by the Kundalini. The practices that awaken Kundalini – meditation, yoga, breathwork – are, in essence, ways to tap into Kali's energy, leading to profound personal and spiritual transformation.

### *The Ethical Implications of Transformation*

As with any powerful force, the energies of Kali and Kundalini must be approached with respect and an understanding of their profound impact. This transformation is not just about personal growth; it's about realizing one's responsibility towards the collective well-being. The ethical use of this energy is essential for it to be a force for positive change in the world.

The journey of awakening and embracing the unified energies of Kali and Kundalini is a path of empowerment, wisdom, and liberation. It is about recognizing and unleashing the divine power within, leading to a life of greater awareness, harmony, and purpose. In this unified energy, lies the potential for not just personal enlightenment but also for contributing to the greater good of the world, aligning oneself with the rhythms of the cosmos and the eternal dance of creation and destruction.

### *The Process of Kundalini Arousal*

Kundalini arousal is not a spontaneous occurrence but a gradual, deliberate process, often facilitated by specific practices such as meditation, pranayama (breath control), yoga and Kali Sadhana as I've personally experienced. This journey requires dedication, discipline, and a deep understanding of the spiritual and physical self. It is a path of both purification and enlightenment, where the practitioner learns to harmonize the body, mind, and spirit.

As Kundalini rises through the chakras, the energy centers of the body, it brings about profound transformation. A rise against gravity is always profound and difficult since it calls for a lot of discipline in daily and mundane life. This process is not merely a personal evolution but a cosmic one, where the individual becomes a conduit for universal energy. The awakening of Kundalini leads to the expansion of consciousness, deepening one's connection with the self and the universe.

### *The Power to Change the World*

The transformation brought about by Kundalini arousal extends beyond personal growth. It imbues one with the power to effect positive change in the world. By tapping into this energy, individuals can create opportunities for themselves and others, fostering a spirit of community, cooperation, and growth. This power becomes a tool for healing, teaching, and enriching the lives around them.

Kundalini awakening also brings with it a profound understanding of the natural elements and the cosmos. Practitioners learn to harness the energies of earth, water, fire, air, and ether, aligning themselves with the rhythms of nature. This harmony with the elements reflects a deeper truth – that the entire cosmos resides within us. As above, so below; as within, so without.

## *The Ethical Use of Kundalini Power*

With great power comes great responsibility. The ethical use of Kundalini energy is paramount. It is not a tool for personal gain at the expense of others but a means to uplift, heal, and harmonize. The true strength of Kundalini lies in its ability to bring about collective well-being and spiritual advancement. It is about realizing our innate potential to bring about transformative change, both within and in the world at large. As we awaken the serpent power within, we step into our role as co-creators of a more harmonious, compassionate, and enlightened world. In harnessing this sacred energy, we not only grow as individuals but also help in the collective evolution of humanity, making the world a sanctuary of peace, understanding, and spiritual abundance.

*Chapter : 7*

# Harnessing the Power of Kali and Her Yoginis: Transforming Energy, Transforming Lives

### *The Cosmic Dance of Energies*

In the grand theatre of the universe, a ceaseless dance of energies unfolds—an eternal symphony where forces of nature create, sustain, and transform existence. Hindu mythology, with its rich tapestry of stories and symbols, brings these forces to life. Among these embodiments of energy, Kali and Her Yoginis stand majestic and profound, representing the dynamic, transformative power inherent in the universe.

### *Kali: The Fierce Divine*

Kali, the fierce manifestation of the Divine Mother, is a figure of awe and reverence. Her imagery, stark and powerful, symbolizes the relentless march of time and the inevitability of change. She is the slayer of negativity, a harbinger of justice, and a beacon of empowerment. In her, the cycle of creation and destruction finds its most vivid representation.

### *The Yoginis: Divine Feminine Forces*

Accompanying Kali are Her Yoginis, each a vibrant thread in the fabric of cosmic energy. These divine entities dance to the primordial rhythms of existence, influencing and balancing the flow of energy across the universe. They are guardians of order, each resonating with unique aspects of the divine feminine—creativity, wisdom, strength, and compassion.

### *Transforming Personal Energies*

Our personal worlds, rife with challenges—be it in finances, career, or relationships—reflect the energies we embody and project. Often, we find ourselves in a web of circumstances that seem beyond our direct control. It is in these moments that the philosophy of Kali and Her Yoginis offers a profound alternative: transforming the energy that envelops these situations.

### *Invoking the Divine*

Inviting Kali and Her Yoginis into our lives is an act of opening ourselves to their transformative influence. It's about aligning with the omnipotent forces they represent, which can catalyze significant shifts in our personal energy fields. This alignment, subtle yet powerful, can bring about remarkable changes in our life situations.

### *Empowerment and Energy Shift*

Through practices centered on empowerment, we channel the essence of the Goddess within. Her energy flows through us, igniting courage and clarity, empowering us to face adversities, strategize effectively, and act decisively. The

Yoginis, in their diverse manifestations, contribute to fostering a milieu of harmony and collaboration.

### The Tools of Transformation

The key to tapping into the power of Kali and Her Yoginis lies in our ability to harness their energies. This is achieved through a blend of spiritual practices—empowering affirmations, visualization, mantra chanting, and ritualistic worship. These practices not only align us with their energies but also initiate a transformative shift within.

### The Ripple Effect of Energy Change

This shift in energy brings about a paradigm shift in our perceptions and interactions. We start to view challenges as opportunities, conflicts as gateways to harmony. This change in energy sets off a domino effect—altering our responses, influencing outcomes, and reshaping our reality.

### A Guide to Transformation

This book is more than just a text; it's a guide to a transformative journey. It offers a roadmap to harness the energies of Kali and Her Yoginis, to initiate a change in the energy around us, and consequently, to metamorphose our lives. It teaches us a fundamental truth: while we may not control every aspect of our lives, we possess the power to alter the energies that surround us. In harnessing the power of Kali and Her Yoginis, we don't just change our energy; we embark on a journey of profound personal transformation.

*Chapter : 8*

# Kali and Her Yoginis: Unleashing the Power Within

In the realm of ancient wisdom and spiritual practices, Kali, the fierce and compassionate Hindu goddess, reigns supreme. She embodies the profound transformation and liberation that can be achieved through the union of physical, mental, and spiritual practices.

Kali and her Yoginis are often misunderstood as dark and destructive deities. However, their true essence lies in helping individuals to tap into their inner strength and potential.

In ancient times, when there was a lack of scientific understanding and technology, people turned to the divine for guidance and support for almost everything. Be it natural calamities or be it childbirth. Kali and her Yoginis were revered as powerful beings who could grant blessings, protection, and aid in personal growth.

### *How can Kali and Her Yoginis help in a person's growth?*

Kali, the fierce form of Devi (Aadi Shakti), is known for her unapologetic boldness and fearlessness. She is often depicted adorned with severed heads and wielding weapons, representing her ability to conquer negativity and ignorance.

Kali's Yoginis, also known as Shaktis, are considered her manifestations and extensions of her power. Each Yogini represents a different aspect of life, such as wisdom, wealth, and protection.

By worshipping Kali and her Yoginis, individuals can tap into their energy and invoke their blessings for specific purposes. For example, worshipping Chamunda Yogini can help in overcoming obstacles, while worshipping Saraswati Yogini can enhance knowledge and creativity.

Moreover, the rituals and practices associated with Kali and her Yoginis involve intense devotion and surrender to the divine. This process helps individuals to let go of their ego and connect with their inner selves, leading to personal growth and self-realisation.

### *Significance in the Ancient Days*

In ancient times, Kali and her Yoginis were revered as protectors and guides. Communities often turned to them for help in difficult situations such as war, famine, or disease. The worship of Kali and her Yoginis also played a significant role in the spiritual growth of individuals, as they were seen as a means to connect with the Supreme.

Furthermore, Kali and her Yoginis were also associated with rituals and practices that helped in unleashing the power within. These practices focused on harnessing one's inner strength and potential, leading to personal growth and enlightenment.

In the ancient era, there was a unique aspect to the worship of Kali and her Yoginis - it was principally a domain of women.

Women, considered embodiments of Shakti or divine feminine power, were seen as being naturally aligned with the energies of Aadi Shakti. These practices allowed them to tap into their inherent strength, helping in unleashing the power within.

The rituals were often held in secret, in secluded spaces away from the gaze of society. Mostly close to a water body, in remote temples in wilderness. The women would gather under the moonlight, chanting mantras and performing rituals that were passed down through generations. This was not merely a form of worship but a means of spiritual self-expression and self-empowerment. It was a tool for women to assert their identity, challenge societal conventions and reclaim their power.

Thus, the worship of Kali and her Yoginis was not just a religious practice but also a radical social movement. It served as a platform for women to unite, express, and empower themselves in a time when their voices were often suppressed. It was through their devotion to Kali and her Yoginis that they found the courage and strength to navigate life's challenges and foster their personal growth. This was the true essence and significance of Kali and her Yoginis in ancient times.

Even today, the teachings and practices associated with Kali and her Yoginis continue to inspire individuals on their journey towards self-discovery and growth. The legacy of Kali and her force lives on, reminding us to honour the divine feminine within ourselves and in the world around us. So, let us continue to learn from these ancient practices and unleash the power within, just as the women of the past did centuries ago. Instead of being confined by societal norms and expectations, let us follow the example set by Kali and her Yoginis and break free from limitations to reach our full potential.

Let us embrace the power within and unleash it to create positive change in our lives and in society. Let us remember that they are not just deities of the past but also powerful symbols of feminine empowerment that can guide us towards a better future. Let their legacy inspire us to honour our own strength and power within to create a life of growth, self-discovery, and empowerment.

## *Kali is not found in Darkness – She is Darkness*

Kali is often perceived as the embodiment of darkness. However, this darkness is not synonymous with evil or malevolence as often portrayed in conventional narratives. Instead, it signifies the profound depths of the unknown, the mysteries of the universe that lie beyond our grasp. Kali, in her dark form, represents the infinite potential that rests in the shadows, the power that can be harnessed when we are willing to confront our deepest fears and insecurities. The darkness of Kali is less about literal absence of light and more about the unlit corridors of self-discovery. It is in this darkness, we encounter our true selves, stripped of pretensions and laid bare in our most authentic form. Therefore, Kali is not just darkness; she is the journey through darkness leading to enlightenment and growth.

Similarly, Kali's Yoginis are not just her companions but also embodiments of her power and strength. Together, they form a powerful force that is unstoppable and uncontainable. They encourage us to embrace our own diversity and complexity, to recognise that we are multifaceted beings capable of greatness and change. The Yoginis represent the different aspects of our personality and the diverse paths we can take towards self-discovery. They remind us that there is no one-size-fits-all approach to growth, but rather, it is a unique journey for each individual that requires self-awareness, courage, and determination.

In ancient times, Kali and her Yoginis were revered as symbols of feminine power, representing the strength and resilience of women. They taught individuals to embrace their innate femininity and harness it as a source of power and wisdom. However, their message is not limited to just one gender; it is applicable to all beings who seek growth and transformation.

Their teachings are more relevant now than ever before, as we navigate through a world that is constantly changing and evolving. In a society where conformity is often valued over individuality, Kali and her Yoginis urge us to break free from societal norms and expectations, to embrace our uniqueness within. By embracing our true selves and all that we are, we open ourselves up to endless possibilities and opportunities for growth.

So, whether you are seeking personal growth, spiritual enlightenment or simply looking to embrace your authentic self, Kali and her Yoginis offer a guiding light on this journey. They remind us that the path to self-discovery may not always be easy, but it is ultimately rewarding and fulfilling. So, let us honour the wisdom of Kali and her Yoginis and embrace our own beauty, strength, and potential as we continue to grow and evolve in this ever-changing world. Let us remember that within each of us lies a powerful force waiting to be unleashed – the divine energy of Kali and her Yoginis.

Chapter : 9

# The Dance of Eternity: Kali and Mahakaal

### *The Enigma of Kali*

In the intricate weave of Hindu mythology, Kali emerges not just as a deity but as a cosmic paradox. She embodies the eternal cycle of birth, life, death, and rebirth, transcending mere mythological figurehead to become a philosophical symbol of the universe's relentless rhythm. Devotees look to her for protection, empowerment, and liberation from the endless cycles of suffering and rebirth. Kali, in her fierce majesty, becomes a potent emblem of feminine strength, a reminder of the universe's intrinsic dance of light and darkness.

### *The Fierce Divine Feminine*

Kali's presence in the Hindu pantheon is deeply rooted, representing the fierce, transformative aspect of the divine feminine. As the ferocious manifestation of Adi Shakti, the primal cosmic energy, she encapsulates the dual nature of creation and destruction. In her iconic depiction, Kali stands with multiple arms, each brandishing symbolic weapon, embodying the roles of creator, preserver, and destroyer.

## The Timeless Nature of Kali

Her name, derived from "kāla," the Sanskrit word for time, signifies her all-encompassing, timeless nature. Kali transcends the mortal realm, representing the nurturing and destructive cycles of the cosmos. Her fierce countenance, with dark or blue-black skin, and a garland of skulls, stands upon the inert form of Lord Shiva, symbolizing the intricate dance of creation and destruction.

Goddess Kali is an embodiment of sensuality and power, an alluring force that commands attention and reverence. Her form is a symphony of curves and shadows, a celebration of feminine strength and beauty that transcends mortal perception.

Her skin, draped in the ethereal hues of midnight, radiates an otherworldly allure. Her body, adorned with the jewels of the cosmos, moves with an intoxicating grace—a dance that echoes the rhythmic heartbeat of the universe. Each movement, a seductive sway, tells a story of divine passion and timeless sensuality.

Her wild, flowing mane of dark tresses cascades like an inky waterfall down her back, entwined with the cosmic secrets of the universe. The strands, like tendrils of desire, seem to whisper ancient truths as they caress the air in the wake of her movements.

Her eyes, pools of deep, hypnotic intensity, hold the mysteries of creation and destruction. Within their depths lies an infinite cosmos of longing and wisdom, a gaze that pierces through the veils of illusion and invites those who dare to look into the abyss of divine desire. As Kali gazes intensely into the cosmic abyss, her eyes ablaze with the fires of divine passion.

Her facial expression, a dance between fierce determination and a subtle, knowing smile, reflects the dual nature of her existence. A protruding tongue, a playful tease that symbolizes the ecstasy of creation, invites those who witness Her to surrender to the intoxicating dance of life and death.

With multiple arms, an intoxicating array, reach out in a divine embrace that captivates the senses. Each limb, adorned with celestial symbols, moves with a fluidity that suggests both power and tenderness—the tender touch of a lover combined with the strength of a cosmic warrior.

In the cosmic embrace of Kali, Her ten limbs extend with a magnetic allure, each limb a mesmerizing blend of sensuality, power, and divine symbolism. Eight of these limbs are adorned with celestial weapons, while the remaining two cradle Mahakaal, the cosmic consort, in a passionate union beneath the goddess.

*AAYUDHA: COSMIC WEAPONS*

*Scimitar of Wisdom (Khadga):*

In one of Kali's arms, a scimitar arcs gracefully, symbolizing the cutting edge of divine knowledge. Its gleaming blade reflects the light of cosmic truths that dispel ignorance.

### *Trident of Cosmic Forces (Trishula):*

Another limb holds a trident, a potent symbol of the three fundamental aspects of existence—creation, preservation, and destruction. Its prongs extend like cosmic tendrils, weaving the intricate dance of cosmic energies.

### *Thunderbolt of Spiritual Strength (Vajra):*

A third arm wields a thunderbolt, a radiant symbol of spiritual strength that illuminates the path of enlightenment. It crackles with the energy of divine realization.

### *Bow and Arrows of Precision (Dhanus and Banas):*

Kali's fourth limb cradles a bow and arrows, representing the focused precision with which she navigates the cosmic dance, hitting the mark of cosmic balance.

### *Conch Shell of Creation (Shankha):*

In another embrace, Kali holds a conch shell, its spirals echoing the sacred vibrations of creation. With each breath, she breathes life into the cosmic symphony.

### *Discus of Cyclical Time (Chakra):*

A sixth limb bears a discus, a symbol of cyclical time and the eternal dance of the cosmos. Its swift rotations embody the perpetual rhythm of existence.

### *Sword of Divine Precision (Asi):*

Kali's seventh arm brandishes a sword, a weapon of divine precision that cuts through illusions, revealing the raw truth that lies beyond.

### *Noose of Cosmic Control (Pasha):*

Another limb extends with a noose, symbolizing Kali's control over the forces that bind the universe. It represents the delicate balance between restraint and liberation.

### *Mahakaal Cradled in Intimate Embrace:*

Two arms, intertwined with Mahakaal, the cosmic consort, engage in an intimate embrace. These limbs hold the essence of passionate connection, an eternal dance of creation that balances nature's forces.

### *Mahakaal in Reclined Repose:*

Lying beneath Kali, Mahakaal, the cosmic consort, reclines in divine surrender. His form represents the timeless, unmanifest potential from which all creation arises, an integral part of the cosmic copulation that sustains the delicate balance of the universe.

Symbol of Divine Harmony: In Mahakaal's reclined surrender, there is a harmony that resonates through the cosmos. It symbolizes the inseparable dance of masculine and feminine energies, where surrender is not a loss but a sublime contribution to the eternal rhythm of creation.

Around Her neck, a necklace of skulls—each a testament to the cycle of life and death—serves as both a macabre adornment and an erotic symbol of the interplay between pleasure and mortality. The jewels that adorn her form sparkle like distant stars, reflecting the cosmic passion that courses through Her being.

Kali's presence is a sensual ode to the cosmic dance, an invitation to explore the depths of desire and the ecstasy of divine connection. In her embrace, the boundaries between the mortal and the divine blur, and the essence of sensuality becomes an integral part of the eternal dance of creation and destruction.

### *Mahakaal as Cosmic Witness:*

While reclining, Mahakaal assumes the role of a cosmic witness—an observer to the unfolding drama of creation and destruction. His presence is a silent acknowledgment of the profound interconnectedness between the cosmic forces.

In this cosmic ballet, Kali's ten limbs create a visual symphony—a dance that encapsulates the dual nature of existence, where divine weapons and passionate embraces converge in the eternal union of creation and destruction.

The union of Kali and Mahakaal transcends physicality, symbolizing the cosmic copulation – an intimate dance of creation where Mahakaal's surrender to Kali's dynamic energy brings forth the ever-changing spectacle of the universe. This sacred union maintains the delicate balance of cosmic energies, where Mahakaal's stillness complements Kali's vibrant motion.

### *Mahakaal: The Timeless One*

Complementing the formidable presence of Kali is Mahakaal, an aspect of Lord Shiva, embodying the concept of time and eternity. Mahakaal is the great destroyer and the ultimate reality, the end point of all creation. He is time in its most relentless form, the devourer of all things, yet also the seed of new beginnings.

In iconography, Mahakaal is often depicted as dark, limitless, and all-encompassing. He is the still point in the cosmic dance, around which Kali moves with fierce grace. Mahakaal's presence is both comforting and terrifying, a reminder of the inevitable cycle of life and death, creation and dissolution.

### *The Dance of Kali and Mahakaal*

The relationship between Kali and Mahakaal is profound and intricate, representing the interplay of dynamic energy and the eternal backdrop of existence. Kali, with her dance of destruction and creation, whirls around the immutable axis that is Mahakaal. Together, they symbolize the cycle of time and the dance of the universe - a balance of movement and stillness, creation and dissolution, life and death.

Their dance is a metaphor for the ebbs and flows of the universe, the perpetual cycle of stars being born and dying, of civilizations rising and falling. Kali's dance is the dance of nature, wild and free, while Mahakaal's stillness is the unchanging reality of time itself.

### *Embracing the Energy of Kali and Mahakaal*

In meditating upon Kali and Mahakaal, one embraces the full spectrum of existence. Kali teaches us to face our fears, to embrace change, and to let go of attachments. Mahakaal reminds us of the impermanence of all things and the constant presence of eternity.

Through understanding Kali and Mahakaal, we come to understand the nature of time, change, and the eternal cycle of the universe. Their energy inspires courage, acceptance, and a profound understanding of the transient yet eternal nature of reality.

Their depiction is not just an artistic or mythological construct; it is a deep philosophical truth about the nature of existence. Through them, we understand the beauty and terror of the universe, the dance of time, and our place within this grand cosmic ballet.

## RITUAL

### *Invoking the Divine: The Ritual of Kali Worship*

In the heart of spiritual awakening, where the veils of the mundane world thin, lies the potent and transformative path of Goddess Kali. This chapter, "Invoking the Divine: The Ritual of Kali Worship," is an odyssey into the depths of ancient traditions, unravelling the profound and often misunderstood facets of Kali, the embodiment of strength, fierceness, and divine femininity.

Our journey begins at the crossroads of reverence and mystery, where the echoes of ancient chants blend with the rhythm of beating drums, leading us into the heart of Kali's worship. Here, the rituals are more than mere ceremonies; they are the gateways to experiencing the raw and powerful aspects of the Divine Feminine. As the night deepens, the air thickens with the scent of incense and the resonance of mantras, each syllable a key unlocking deeper spiritual truth.

In this sacred space, we will explore the intricate rituals dedicated to Kali, beginning with the purifying flames of fire cleansing and culminating in the profound recitation of the Sahasranama. These rituals, steeped in centuries of tradition, are not just acts of devotion but pathways to transcendence, offering a glimpse into the eternal dance of creation, preservation, and destruction.

As you turn these pages, you will be introduced to the symbolic significance of each element of the ritual, from the preparation of the altar to the final offerings. We will delve into the meanings behind the mantras and stotras, uncovering layers of symbolism embedded in these ancient verses. The "Kalika Stotram," a hymn of unparalleled depth, will be a focal point, its resonance versus a guiding light in our exploration.

This chapter is not just a guide; it is an invitation to experience the transformative power of Kali's worship. It beckons you to immerse yourself in the ritual, to let the rhythms and chants permeate your being, and to emerge with a deeper understanding of the Divine and of yourself.

As we embark on this journey, let us approach with an open heart and mind, ready to embrace the mysteries and blessings of Kali, the Dark Mother, in her most profound and sacred form.

## *1. Preparation Phase*

Purification of Self and Space: Begin with self-purification (snana) and cleansing the ritual space using sacred herbs or incense.

Creation of Sacred Altar: Erect an altar for Goddess Kali, adorning it with her images, symbols (like the trident or sword), and dark-coloured drapery.

Gathering of Offerings: Prepare offerings like red flowers, incense, food, and lamps. Include items symbolizing Kali's fierce aspect, like red hibiscus.

## *2. Invocation of Goddess Kali*

Mantra Chanting: Chant "Om Krim Kalikayai Namah" or other Kali mantras to invoke her energy.

Kali Stotra: Recite a chosen Kali Stotra (hymn), like the "Kali Kavacham" or "Mahakali Stotram", invoking various attributes and forms of the Goddess.

### 3. Fire Cleansing Ritual (Homa)

Igniting the Sacred Fire: Light a ceremonial fire, reciting blessings to invoke the fire god, Agni.

Offerings to Fire: Offer ghee, herbs, grains, and other sacred items into the fire while chanting Kali-specific mantras.

Fire Meditation: Focus on the fire, visualizing it burning away all negativity and obstacles.

### 4. Deep Meditation and Internalization

Lead a meditation focusing on internalizing Kali's qualities of strength, transformation, and liberation.

### Kali Dhyanam – Meditation on Goddess Kali

Sit in a quiet and comfortable space, allowing the external world to fade away as you turn your focus inward. Take deep, slow breaths to centre your mind and relax your body. As you ease into a state of calmness, begin to visualize a sacred space around you, a realm where the Divine presence of Kali can be felt.

### Invocation

With reverence in your heart, invoke the presence of Goddess Kali. Chant softly, "Om Krim Kalikayai Namah," letting the mantra resonate within you, creating a sacred space for her energy.

### Visualizing the Goddess

In the eye of your mind, visualize the magnificent form of Kali. She stands powerful and resplendent, her complexion dark as the night sky, embodying the boundless cosmos. Her eyes, fiery and penetrating, see through all illusions, offering both the wisdom of the ages and the compassion of the mother.

Kali's long, untamed hair flows like a river of freedom, symbolizing her unbound nature. She wears a garland of severed heads, each representing a conquered ego, and a skirt of dismembered arms, signifying the detachment from material possessions and deeds.

In her four arms, she wields symbols of her power: a sword of divine knowledge, a severed head representing the ego cut away by wisdom, a bowl catching the nectar of immortality, and a gesture of fearlessness and blessing.

### *Embracing Kali's Energy*

Feel the powerful energy of Kali surrounding you. Her aura is intense and transformative, yet within her ferocity lies deep love and compassion. As you meditate on her form, embrace the qualities she embodies - fearlessness, strength, empowerment, and the transformative power of change.

Contemplate the teachings of Kali. She reminds us of the impermanence of life and the importance of spiritual liberation. Her fierce form teaches us to confront our fears and limitations, guiding us towards the path of truth and enlightenment.

As your meditation deepens, feel a profound connection with Kali. Let her strength infuse your being, her wisdom enlighten your mind, and her compassion warm your heart. Slowly, when you are ready, bring your awareness back to the present moment, carrying with you the blessings and insights from this sacred meditation.

Please consider reading the Original Dakshina Kali Dhyanam during practice.

This Kali Dhyanam is designed to guide the practitioner into a deep, meditative state, fostering a connection with the divine energy of Kali. It can be used as part of a ritual, as a standalone meditation, or as a way to deepen one's spiritual practice. Reflect on her teachings about life, death, and spiritual awakening.

## *5. Recitation of Stotras and Scriptures*

"Kali Tandava Stotram" or "Kali Sahasranamam".

Kali Sahasranama: Recite the thousand names of Kali, a profound act of devotion and connection with the Goddess.

## *6. Closing Ritual*

Dissolution of the Ritual Space: Gently put out the fire, dismantle the altar, and respectfully dispose of or store the ritual items. Offer a closing prayer, expressing gratitude to Kali for her protection, guidance, and blessings. (Always better to write your own)

## *7. Integration and Reflection*

Journaling and Personal Reflection: Encourage writing down personal experiences, dreams, or visions related to the ritual.

Additional Considerations: Ensure the ritual respects the cultural and religious origins of Kali worship. If conducted in a group, encourage active participation in chants, readings, and offerings.

Always maintain safety, especially during the fire ritual.

This extended ritual is designed to be immersive and comprehensive, respecting traditional practices while allowing for personal spiritual exploration.

*Chapter : 10*

# Kali Sahasranama

1. Smasanakalika: She who removes darkness from the cremation grounds or from death.
2. Kali: She who removes darkness.
3. Bhadrakali: She who is the docile remover of darkness.
4. Kapalini: She who bears the skulls of impurity.
5. Guhyakali: She who is the hidden or secretive remover of darkness.
6. MahaKali: She who is the great remover of darkness.
7. Kurukullavirodhini: She who confronts the forces of duality.
8. Kalika: She who is the cause of removing darkness.
9. Kalaratrisca: She who is the dark night of ignorance.
10. Mahakalanitambini: She who is the eternal mother of great time.
11. Kalabhairavabharya ca: She who is the consort of the fearfulness of infinite time.
12. Kulavartmaprakasini: She who illuminates the complete family tree.
13. Kamada: She who is the giver of all desire.
14. Kamini: She who is the giver of this desire.
15. Kamya: She who is desired.

16. Kamaniyasvabhavini: She who is the intrinsic nature of that which is desired.
17. Kasturirasaliptangi: She whose limbs are anointed with the juice of musk.
18. Kunjaresvaragamini: She who moves like the lord of elephants.
19. Kakaravarnasarvangi: She who is all the limbs of the letter "ka," the cause.
20. Kamini: She who is this desire.
21. Kamasundari: She who is beautiful desire.
22. Kamarta: She who is the object of desire.
23. Kamarupa ca: She who is the form of desire.
24. Kamadhenuh: She who is the cow that fulfills all desires.
25. Kalavati: She who is the repository of all qualities or arts.
26. Kanta: She who is beauty enhanced by love.
27. Kamasvarupa ca: She who is the intrinsic form of desire.
28. Kamakhya: She whose name is desire.
29. Kulapalini: She who protects excellence.
30. Kulina: She who is excellence.
31. Kulavatyamba: She who is the repository of excellence.
32. Durga: She who is the reliever of difficulties.
33. Durgartinasini: She who is the destroyer of all various difficulties.
34. Kumari: She who is ever pure.
35. Kulaja: She who gives birth to excellence.
36. Krsna: She who manifests all action.
37. Krsnadeha: She who has a dark body.

38. Krsodara: She who holds aloft all action.
39. Krsamgi: She who embodies all actions.
40. Kulisamgi ca: She who is the embodiment of excellence.
41. Krimkari: She who causes dissolution of the subtle body into the causal body.
42. Kamala: She who is lotus (Lakshmi).
43. Kala: She who is art or all attributes.
44. Karalasya: She who has a gaping mouth.
45. Karali ca: She who dissolves all into her being.
46. Kulakanta-parajita: She whose excellent beauty is undefeated.
47. Ugra: She who is terrible.
48. Ugraprabha: She whose light is terrible.
49. Dipta: She who is light.
50. Vipracitta: She whose objects of consciousness are varied.
51. Mahanana: She who has a great face.
52. Nilaghana: She who has the complexion of a dark cloud.
53. Valaka ca: She who exemplifies the freedom of a swan.
54. Matra: She who is verse.
55. Mudramitasita: She whose positions of her limbs are extremely elegant.
56. Brahmi: She who is creative energy.
57. Narayani: She who is the exposure of consciousness.
58. Bhadra: She who is excellent.
59. Subhadra: She who is the excellent of excellence.
60. Bhaktavatsala: She who nourishes all devotees.
61. Mahesvari ca: She who is the great seer of all.

62. Camunda: She who moves in the paradigm of consciousness.
63. Varahi: She who is the boar of sacrifice.
64. Narasimhika: She who is the ferocious half-human, half-lion of courage.
65. Vajrangi: She who has limbs of lightning.
66. Vajrakankali: She whose head shines like lightning.
67. Nrmundasragvini: She who is adorned by a garland.
68. Siva: She who is the energy of the consciousness of infinite goodness.
69. Malini: She who wears a garland of skulls.
70. Naramundali: She who holds the head of a man.
71. Galatrudhirabhusana: From the garland of skulls around her neck, falls drops of blood.
72. Ratkacandanasiktangi: She whose limbs are covered by red.
73. Sindurarunamastaka: She whose forehead is marked with the vermilion of love which brings the light of wisdom.
74. Ghorarupa: She who is of fearful form.
75. Ghoradamstra: She whose teeth are fearful.
76. Ghoraghoratara: She who is auspicious, which takes beyond inauspiciousness.
77. Subha: She who is pure.
78. Mahadamstra: She who has great teeth.
79. Mahamaya: She who is the great definition of consciousness.
80. Sundanti: She who has excellent teeth.
81. Yugadantura: She who is beyond the ages of time.
82. Sulocana: She who has beautiful eyes.

83. Virupaksi: She whose eyes are of indescribable form.
84. Visalaksi: She who has great eyes.
85. Trilocana: She who has three eyes.
86. Saradenduprasannasya: She who is pleased as the autumn moon.
87. Sphuratsmerambujeksana: She who's purity shines in her lotus eyes.
88. Attahasaprasannasya: She who has a great laugh in extreme pleasure.
89. Smeravaktra: She who speaks words of remembrance.
90. Subhasini: She who has excellent expression.
91. Prasannapadmavadana: She whose lotus lips smile.
92. Smitasya: She whose face is always happy.
93. Piyabhasini: She who is the beloved expression of love.
94. Kotaraksi: She whose eyes are infinite.
95. Kulasresta: She who is the excellent of excellence or of excellent family.
96. Mahati: She who has a great mind.
97. Bahubhasini: She who has various expressions.
98. Sumatih: She who has an excellent mind.
99. Kumatih: She who has a devious mind.
100. Canda: She who has passion; worlds consider the universe.
101. Candamundativegini: She who destroys passion, meanness, and other negativities.
102. Pracandacandika: She who is greatly terrible passion.
103. Candi: She who tears apart thoughts.
104. Candika: She who is the cause of tearing apart all thought.

105. Candavegini: She who destroys all passion.
106. Sukesi: She who has beautiful hair.
107. Muktakesi ca: She who has unbound hair.
108. Dirghakesi: She who has long hair.
109. Mahatkuca: She who has large breasts.
110. Pretadehakarnapura: She who has the ears of the cosmic body.
111. Pratapanisumekhala: She who has the hands and waist of the cosmic body.
112. Pretasana: She who sits with disembodied spirits.
113. Priyapreta: She who is the beloved of disembodied spirits.
114. Pretabhumikrtalaya: She who is the land where disembodied spirits reside.
115. Smasanavasini: She who resides in the cremation grounds.
116. Punya: She who is merit.
117. Punyada: She who is the giver of merit.
118. Kulapandita: She who is the one of excellent knowledge.
119. Punyalaya: She who is the residence of merit.
120. Punyadeha: She who embodies merit.
121. Punyasloka ca: She who every utterance is merit.
122. Pavini: She who blows like a fresh breeze.
123. Puta: She who is the daughter.
124. Pavitra: She who is pure.
125. Parama: She who is supreme.
126. Purapunyavibhusana: She who illuminates the fullest merit.
127. Punyanamni: She whose name is meritorious.
128. Bhitihara: She who takes away fear and doubt.
129. Varada: She who is the grantor of boons.

130. Khangapalini: She who has the sword of wisdom in her hand.
131. Nrmundahastasasta ca: She who holds the skull of impure thought.
132. Chinnamasta: She who holds the severed head of duality.
133. Sunasika: She who has an excellent organ of scent.
134. Daksina: She who looks to the south; she who is the offering made in respect for guidance.
135. Syamala: She who has a dark complexion.
136. Syama: She who is dark.
137. Santa: She who is peace.
138. Pinonnatastani: She who raises the trident in her hands.
139. Digambara: She who wears space.
140. Srkkanta: She whose beauty creates.
141. Raktavahini: She who is the vehicle of passion.
142. Ghorarava: She whose sound is terrible.
143. Sivasamgi: She who is with Shiva.
144. Visamgi: She who is without any other.
145. Madanatura: She who is the ultimate intoxication.
146. Matta: She who is the great mind or thinker.
147. Pramatta: She who is the foremost mind or thinker.
148. Pramada: She who is the giver of preeminence.
149. Sudhasindhunivasini: She who resides in the ocean of purity.
150. Atimatta: She who is extremely great mind.
151. Mahamatta: She who is the great mind.
152. Sarvakarsanakarini: She who is the cause of all attraction.

153. Gitapriya: She who is the beloved of songs.
154. Vadyarata: She who is extremely pleased by music.
155. Pretanrtyaparayana: She who is the eternal dance of disembodied spirits.
156. Caturbhuja: She who has four arms.
157. Dasabhuja: She who has ten arms.
158. Astadasabhuja tatha: She who has eighteen arms also.
159. Katyayani: She who is ever pure.
160. Jaganmata: She who is the mother of the perceivable universe.
161. Jagatam Paramesvari: She who is the supreme ruler of the perceivable universe.
162. Jagadhandhuh: She who is the friend of the perceivable universe.
163. Jagaddhatri: She who creates the perceivable universe.
164. Jagadanandakarini: She who is the cause of bliss in the perceivable universe.
165. Jagajjivamayi: She who is the manifestation of all life in the universe.
166. Haimavati: She who is born of the Himalayas.
167. Maya: She who is the great measurement of consciousness.
168. Mahamahi: She who is the great expression.
169. Nagayajnopavitangi: She who is the sacred thread on the body of the snake, the adornment of Kundalini.
170. Nagini: She who is the snake.
171. Nagasayini: She who rests on snakes.
172. Nagakanya: She who is the daughter of the snake.
173. Devakanya: She who is the daughter of the gods.

174. Gandharvi: She who sings celestial divine tunes.
175. Kinnaresvari: She who is the supreme ruler of heavenly beings.
176. Moharatrih: She who is the night of ignorance.
177. Maharatrih: She who is the great nights.
178. Daruna: She who supports all.
179. Bhasvarasuri: She whose radiance destroys duality.
180. Vidyadhari: She who grants great knowledge.
181. Vasumati: She who has wealth.
182. Yaksini: She who gives wealth.
183. Yogini: She who is always in union.
184. Jara: She who is old.
185. Raksasi: She who is the mother of all demons.
186. Dakini: She who is the female demonic being.
187. Vedamayi: She who is the expression of wisdom.
188. Vedavibhusana: She who illuminates wisdom.
189. Srutih: She who is that which has been heard.
190. Smrtih: She who is that which is remembered.
191. Mahavidya: She who is great knowledge.
192. Guhyavidya: She who is hidden knowledge.
193. Puratani: She who is the oldest.
194. Cintya: She who is thought.
195. Acintya: She who is unthinkable.
196. Svadha: She who is oblations of ancestral praise.
197. Svaha: She who is oblations of "I am one with God."
198. Nidra: She who is sleep.
199. Tandra ca: She who is partially awake.

200. Parvati: She who is the Daughter of the Mountain.
201. Aparna: She who is Without Parts.
202. Niscala: She who cannot be divided.
203. Lola: She who has a Protruding Tongue.
204. Sarvadidya: She who is All Knowledge.
205. Tapasvini: She who is the Performer of Purifying Austerities.
206. Ganga: She who is the Holy River.
207. Kasi: She who is Benaras.
208. Saci: She who is the Wife of Indra.
209. Sita: She who is the Wife of Rama.
210. Sati: She who is the Wife of Siva.
211. Satyaparayana: She who always moves in truth.
212. Nitih: She who is Systematized Knowledge or Method.
213. Sunitih: She who is Excellent Systematized Knowledge.
214. Surucih: She who is Excellent Taste.
215. Tustih: She who is Satisfaction.
216. Pustih: She who is Nourishment.
217. Dhrtih: She who is Consistent Solidity.
218. Ksama: She who is Forgiveness.
219. Vani: She who is Words.
220. Buddhih: She who is Intelligence.
221. Mahalaksmih: She who is the Great Goal of Existence.
222. Laksmih: She who is the Goal.
223. Nilasarasvati: She who is the Blue Goddess of Knowledge.
224. Srotasvati: She who is the Spirit of All Sounds.

225. Sarasvati: She who is the Personification of One's Own Ocean of Existence.
226. Matamgi: She who is the Mother of All Bodies.
227. Vijaya: She who is Conquest.
228. Jaya: She who is Victory.
229. Nadi Sindhuh: She who is Rivers and Oceans.
230. Sarvamayi: She who is the Expressions of All.
231. Tara: She who is the Illuminator.
232. Sunyanivasini: She who resides in Silence.
233. Suddha: She who is Purity.
234. Tarangini: She who makes Waves.
235. Medha: She who is the Intellect of Love.
236. Lakini: She who is Manifested Energies.
237. Bahurupini: She who has Many Forms.
238. Sthula: She who is the Gross Body.
239. Suksma: She who is Subtle.
240. Suksmatara: She who is the Subtle Wave.
241. Bhagavati: She who is the Female Ruler of All.
242. Anuragini: She who is the Feeling of Emotions.
243. Paramanandarupa ca: She who is the Form of Supreme Bliss.
244. Cidanandasvarupini: She who is the Intrinsic Nature of the Bliss of Consciousness.
245. Sarvanandamayi: She who is the Expression of All Bliss.
246. Nitya: She who is Eternal.
247. Sarvanandasvarupini: She who is the Intrinsic Nature of All Bliss.

248. Subhada: She who is Giver of Purity.
249. Nandini: She who is Blissful.
250. Stutya: She who is Praise.
251. Stavaniyasvabhavani: She who is the Intrinsic Nature of Songs of Prayers.
252. Ramkini: She who Manifests Subtlety.
253. Bhamkini: She who is Ferocious.
254. Citra: She who is Artistic.
255. Vicitra: She who has Various Artistic Capacities.
256. Citrarupini: She who is the Form of All Art.
257. Padma: She who is the Lotus.
258. Padmalaya: She who Resides in a Lotus.
259. Padmamukhi: She who has Lotus Mouth.
260. Padmavibhusana: She who Shines like a Lotus.
261. Hakini: She is the Energy of the Divine "I."
262. Sakini: She who is the Energy of Peace.
263. Santa: She who is Peace.
264. Rakini: She who is the Energy of Subtlety.
265. Rudhirapriya: She who is the Beloved.
266. Bhrantih: She who is Confusion.
267. Bhavani: She who is Manifested Existence.
268. Rudrani: She who is the Energy that Removes Sufferings.
269. Mrdani: She who is the Rhythm of Life.
270. Satrumardini: She who is the Destroyer of All Enmity.
271. Upendrani: She who is the Highest Energy of the Ruler of the Pure.

272. Mahendrani: She who is the Great Energy of the Ruler of the Pure.
273. Jyotsna: She who Radiates Light.
274. Candrasvarupini: She who is the Intrinsic Nature of the Moon of Devotions.
275. Suryarmika: She who is the Soul of the Light of Wisdom.
276. Rudrapatni: She who is the Wife of Rudra, the Reliever of Sufferings.
277. Raudri: She who is Fierce.
278. Stri Prakrtih: She who is the Woman of Nature or the Nature of Women.
279. Puman: She who is Masculine.
280. Saktih: She who is Energy.
281. Suktih: She who is Happiness.
282. Matih: She who is the Mind.
283. Mata: She who is the Mother.
284. Bhuktih: She who is Enjoyment.
285. Muktih: She who is Liberation.
286. Pativrata: She who Observes the Vows of Devotion to her Husband.
287. Sarvesvari: She who is the Supreme Ruler of All.
288. Sarvamata: She who is Mother of All.
289. Sarvani: She who Dwells in All.
290. Haravallabha: She who is Siva's Strength.
291. Sarvajna: She who is Knower of All.
292. Siddhida: She who is Giver of the Attainment of Perfection.

293. Siddha: She who has Attained Perfection.
294. Bhavya: She who is Existence.
295. Bhavya: She who is All Attitudes.
296. Bhayapaha: She who is Beyond all Fear.
297. Kartri: She who Creates.
298. Hartri: She who Transforms or Destroys.
299. Palayitri: She who Protects
300. Sarvari: She who gives rest.
301. Tamasi: She who manifests darkness.
302. Daya: She who is compassionate.
303. Tamisra: She who mixes or mingles.
304. Tamasi: She who manifests darkness.
305. Sthanuh: She who is established.
306. Sthira: She who is still.
307. Dhira: She who is stationary.
308. Tapasvini: She who performs austerities.
309. Carvangi: She whose body is in motion.
310. Cancala: She who is restless.
311. Lolajihva: She who has a protruding tongue.
312. Carucaritrini: She whose character is to heal.
313. Trapa: She who saves from fear.
314. Trapavati: She whose spirit saves from fear.
315. Lajja: She who is modesty.
316. Vilajja: She who is without modesty.
317. Hrih: She who is humble.
318. Rajovati: She who is the repository of Rajas Guna.

319. Sarasvati: She who is the personification of one's own ocean.
320. Dharmanistha: She who is the strict observance of the ideals of perfection.
321. Srestha: She who is ultimate.
322. Nisthuranadini: She whose vibration is extremely subtle.
323. Garistha: She who is always happy to see her devotees.
324. Dustasamhartri: She who dissolves all evil.
325. Visista: She who is especially beloved.
326. Sreyasi: She who is the ultimate.
327. Ghrna: She who is hatred.
328. Bhima: She who is terribly fierce.
329. Bhayanaka: She who is extremely fearful.
330. Bhimanadini: She who has a fierce roar.
331. Bhih: She who is fierce.
332. Prabhavati: She who is the spirit of illumination.
333. Vagisvari: She who is the supreme ruler of all vibrations.
334. Srih: She who is respect.
335. Yamuna: She who manifests complete control.
336. Yajnakartri: She who is the performer of union or sacrifice.
337. Yajuhpriya: She who is the beloved of union or lover of Yajur Veda.
338. Rksamarthavanilaya: She who resides in the three Vedas.
339. Ragini: She who is all rhythm.
340. Sobhanasvara: She who is the supreme ruler of illumination.
341. Kalakanthi: She who has a dark throat.

342. Kambukanthi: She whose neck has lines like a conch shell.
343. Venuvinaparayana: She who is always playing the vina instruments.
344. Vamsini: She for whom all is family.
345. Vaisnavi: She who pervades the universe.
346. Svaccha: She who desires herself.
347. Dharitri: She who holds the three.
348. Jagadisvari: She who is the supreme ruler of the perceivable universe.
349. Madhumati: She who is the nectar of honey.
350. Kundalini: She who is the manifestation of individual energy.
351. Rddhih: She who is prosperity.
352. Siddhih: She who is the attainment of perfection.
353. Sucismita: She who is the remembrance of the pure.
354. Rambhorvasi: She who is the apsaras Rambha and Urvasi.
355. Rati Rama: She who is extremely beautiful.
356. Rohini: She who is the luminous light of the heavens.
357. Sankhini: She who holds a conch shell.
358. Magha: She who is infinite wealth.
359. Revati: She who is abundance.
360. Cakrini: She who holds a discus.
361. Krsna: She who is dark, she who is the performer of all actions.
362. Gadini: She who holds a club.
363. Padmini Tatha: She who is a lotus then.
364. Sulini: She who holds a spear.

365. Parighastra ca: She who holds the weapon of good actions.
366. Pasini: She who holds the net.
367. Samgapanini: She who holds the bow named Samga in her hands.
368. Pinakadharini: She who holds the spear.
369. Dhumra: She who obscures perceptions.
370. Sarabhi: She whose strength is greater than lions or elephants.
371. Vanamalini: She who is the gardener of the forest.
372. Rathini: She who conveys all.
373. Samaraprita: She who loves the battle.
374. Vegini: She who is swift.
375. Ranapandita: She who is expert in war.
376. Jatini: She who has disheveled hair.
377. Vajrini: She who holds the thunderbolt or lightning.
378. Lila: She who is the divine drama.
379. Iavanyambudhicandrika: She whose beauty radiated the light of knowledge.
380. Balipriya: She who is the beloved of sacrifice.
381. Sadapujya: She who is worthy of worship.
382. Purna: She who is full, complete, perfect.
383. Daityendramathini: She who is welcomed by the leader of all Asuras.
384. Mahisasurasamhartri: She who is destroyer of the great ruler of duality.
385. Kamini: She who is all desires.
386. Raktadantika: She who has red teeth.

387. Raktapa: She who protects passion.
388. Rudhiraktangi: She whose body is covered with passion.
389. Raktakharparahastini: She who bears a cup of passion in her hands.
390. Raktapriya: She whose loves, or is the beloved of passion.
391. Mamsarucirasavasaktamanasa: She who delights in eating meat and drinking intoxicating spirits.
392. Galacchonitamundali: She who wears a garland of heads dripping blood.
393. Kanthamalavibhusana: She who wears a garland upon her neck.
394. Savasana: She who sits upon a corpse.
395. Citantahstha: She who is established in the ultimate consciousness.
396. Mahesi: She who is the greatest seer of all.
397. Vrsavahini: She who rides upon the bull of determination.
398. Vyaghratvagambara: She who wears a garment of tiger skin.
399. Cinacailini: She who moves with the speed of a deer.
400. Simhavahini: She who rides upon a lion.
401. Vamadevi: She who is the beloved goddess.
402. Mahadevi: She who is a great goddess.
403. Gauri: She who is rays of light.
404. Sarvajnabhamini: She who illuminates all wisdom.
405. Balika: She who is a young girl.
406. Taruni: She who is a middle-aged lady.
407. Vrddha: She who is an old lady.

408. Vrddhamata: She who is the mother of the aged.
409. Aratura: She who is beyond age.
410. Subhruh: She who has an excellent forehead.
411. Vilasini: She who resides within herself.
412. Brahmavadini: She who is the vibration of the supreme deity.
413. Brahmani: She who creates divinity.
414. Mahi: She who is Earth.
415. Svapnavati: She who is the spirit of dreams.
416. Citralekha: She who is various writings.
417. Lopamudra: She who is the manifestation of that which is beyond manifested existence.
418. Suresvari: She who is the supreme ruler of all divinity.
419. Amogha: She who is always rewarding.
420. Arundhati: She who is the purity of devotion, epitome of commitment.
421. Tiksna: She who is sharp.
422. Bhogavati: She who is the spirit of all enjoyment.
423. Anuragini: She who is the spirit of all feelings.
424. Mandakini: She who organizes the mind to optimum efficiency.
425. Mandahasa: She whose mind always laughs.
426. Jvalamukhi: She whose face radiates.
427. Asurantaka: She who is the cause of the end of the forces of duality.
428. Manada: She who is the giver of discipline.
429. Manini: She who creates discipline.

430. Manya: She who is discipline.
431. Mananiya: She who is the supreme lord of discipline.
432. Madatura: She who is completely intoxicated.
433. Madira Meduronmada: She who is intoxicated with divine spirit.
434. Medhya: She who is born of intellect.
435. Sadhya: She who is the performer of all discipline.
436. Prasadini: She who is the prasada or consecration of offerings.
437. Sumadhyanantagunini: She who resides in the middle of infinite excellent qualities.
438. Sarvalokottamottama: All the beings of all the worlds consider her to be greater than the greatest.
439. Jayada: She who is the giver of victory.
440. Jitvara: She who grants the boon of victory.
441. Jetri: She who is victorious over the three.
442. Jayasrih: She who is victorious with respect.
443. Jayasalini: She who is the repository of victory.
444. Subhada: She who is the giver of purity.
445. Sukhada: She who is the giver of happiness or comfort.
446. Satya: She who is the manifestation of truth.
447. Sabhasamksobhakarini: She who is the cause of purity for the entire community.
448. Sivaduti: She for whom Siva is the ambassador.
449. Bhutimati: She who is the expression of all manifested existence.
450. Vibhutih: She who is the expression of the expressionless deity.

451. Bhisananana: She whose face is free from fear.
452. Kaumari: She who is the manifestation of the ever-pure one.
453. Kulaja: She who is the giver of birth to the family.
454. Kunti: She who takes away the deficiency of others.
455. Kulastri: She who is the woman of the family.
456. Kulapalika: She who is the protector of the family.
457. Kirttih: She who is fame.
458. Yasasvini: She who is welfare.
459. Bhusa: She who is the peace of all beings.
460. Bhustha: She who is the cause of peace to all beings.
461. Bhutapatipriya: She who is loved by the lord of all disembodied spirits.
462. Saguna: She who is with qualities.
463. Nirguna: She who is without qualities.
464. Trsna: She who is all thirst.
465. Nistha: She who obeys all the rules.
466. Kastha: She who is the cause of desire.
467. Pratisthita: She who establishes.
468. Dhanistha: She who is the beloved wealth.
469. Dhanada: She who is the giver of wealth.
470. Dhanya: She who is wealthy.
471. Vasudha: She who supports the Earth.
472. Suprakasini: She who is excellent illumination.
473. Urvi: She who is the supreme lord of circumstances.
474. Gurvi: She who is the supreme lord of gurus.
475. Gurusrestha: She who is the ultimate guru.

476. Sadguna: She who is with qualities of truth.
477. Trigunatmika: She who is the manifestation of the soul of the three qualities.
478. Rajnamajna: She who is the wisdom of the order of the king.
479. Mahaprajna: She who is the great ultimate wisdom.
480. Saguna: She who is with qualities.
481. Nirgunatmika: She who is the manifestation of the soul of the three qualities.
482. Mahakulina: She who is the mother of all the great family.
483. Niskama: She who is without desire.
484. Sakama: She who is with desire.
485. Kamajivani: She who is the life of desire.
486. Kamadevakala: She who is the attributes of the lord of desire.
487. Ramabhirama: She who is the energy of perfection in the subtle body.
488. Sivanartaki: She who dances with Siva.
489. Cinttamanih: She who is the jewel of all thought.
490. Kalpalata: She who clings to thought.
491. Jagrati: She who wakes up the universe.
492. Dinavatsala: She who is the refuge of the downtrodden.
493. Karttiki: She who is the expression of all that is done.
494. Krtika: She who is the doer or the cause of all doing.
495. Krtya: She who is that which is done.
496. Ayodhya Visamasama: She who is the same as the place where there is no war.

497. Sumantra: She who is the excellent mantra which takes away the mind.
498. Mantrini: She who is the energy of all mantras.
499. Purna: She who is perfect.
500. Hladini: She who is always happy.
501. Klesanasini: She who is the destroyer of all imperfections.
502. Trailokyajanani: She who is the mother of all the three worlds.
503. Jyestha: She who is the oldest.
504. Mimamsamantrarupini: She who is the intrinsic nature of Vedic knowledge.
505. Tadaganimnajathara: She who is the fire of all digestion.
506. Suskamamsasthimalini: She who wears a garland of dried limbs.
507. Avantimathurahrdya: She who is the heart of Mathura and Avadha.
508. Trailokyapavanaksama: She who brings the winds of forgiveness to the three worlds.
509. Vyaktavyaktatmika murtih: She who is the image of the manifest and unmanifested soul.
510. Sarabhi bhimanadini: She whose sound is extremely loud.
511. Ksemankari: She who is the welfare of all.
512. Sankari ca: She who is the cause of peace.
513. Sarvasammohakarini: She who is ignorance of all.
514. Urdhvatejasvini: She who is the rising light of all.
515. Klinna: She whose heart is very soft.
516. Mahatejasvini tatha: She who is the great light.

517. Advaitabhogini: She who enjoys non-duality.
518. Pujya: She who is worthy of worship.
519. Yuvati: She who is young.
520. Sarvamangala: She who is all welfare.
521. Sarvapriyankari: She who is the cause of all love.
522. Bhogya: She who is enjoyed.
523. Dharani: She who supports all.
524. Pisitasana: She who sits upon a deer.
525. Bhayamkari: She who is fearful.
526. Papahara: She who takes away all sins.
527. Niskalamka: She who is without fault.
528. Vasamkari: She who controls.
529. Asa: She who is hope.
530. Trsna: She who is thirst.
531. Candrakala: She who is the digit of the moon, attribute of devotion.
532. Indrani: She who is the energy of the ruler of the pure.
533. Vayuvegini: She who moves with the freedom of emancipation.
534. Sahasrasuryasamkasa: She whose illumination is like a thousand suns.
535. Candrakotisamaprabha: She whose illumination is like ten million moons.
536. Nisumbhasumbhasamhantri: She who dissolves self-deprecation and self-conceit.
537. Raktabijavinasini: She who is the destroyer of the seed of desire.

538. Madhukaitabhahantri ca: She who dissolves too much and too little.
539. Mahisasuraghatini: She who is the destroyer of the great ego.
540. Vahnimandalamadhyastha: She who is situated in the middle of the circle of fire.
541. Sarvasattvapratisthita: She who establishes all truth.
542. Sarvacaravati: She who is the spirit of all that does not move.
543. Sarvadevakanyadhidevata: She who is the supreme goddess of all divine females.
544. Daksakanya: She who is the daughter of ability.
545. Daksayajnanasini: She who is the destroyer of the sacrifice of ability.
546. Durgatarini: She who is the reliever of difficulties, who takes us across the ocean of objects and relationships.
547. Ijya: She who is desired.
548. Pujya: She who is worthy of worship.
549. Satkirttih: She who is true fame.
550. Brahmarupini: She who has the capacity of the form of supreme divinity.
551. Vibhirbhutih: She who manifests the greatest fears.
552. Rambhotuh: She who is the beautiful one residing in the thighs.
553. Caturakara: She who manifests the four of creation.
554. Jayanti: She who is victory.
555. Karuna: She who is compassionate.
556. Kuhuh: She who is the new moon.

557. Manasvini: She who reflects mind.
558. Devamata: She who is mother of gods.
559. Yasasya: She who is worthy of welfare.
560. Brahmacarini: She who moves in the supreme consciousness.
561. Siddhida: She who is the giver of perfection.
562. Vrddhida: She who is the giver of change or modification.
563. Vrddhih: She who is change or modification.
564. Sarvadya: She who is foremost of all; she who is before all.
565. Sarvadayini: She who is the giver of all.
566. Agadharupini: She who is the intrinsic nature of that which does not end.
567. Dhyeya: She who is meditated upon.
568. Muladharanivasini: She who resides in the Muladhara Cakra.
569. Ajna: She who orders creation.
570. Prajna: She who is primordial wisdom.
571. Purnamanah: She who is full and complete.
572. Candramukhyanukulini: She who is the complete collection of the face of the moon.
573. Vavaduka: She who charms everyone with her speech.
574. Nimnanabhih: She whose navel is indented.
575. Satyasandha: She who has found truth.
576. Drdhavrata: She who is determined in her vow.
577. Anvisiki: She who embodies all spiritual knowledge.
578. Dandaniti: She who is the punishment by which discipline is prescribed.

579. Trayi: She who is three.
580. Tridivasundari: She who is the beauty of the three divinities.
581. Jvalini: She who burns.
582. Jvalini: She who causes to burn.
583. Sailatanaya: She who is the daughter of the mountain.
584. Vindhyavasini: She who resides in mountains of knowledge that breed humility.
585. Pratyaya: She who sees all concepts.
586. Khecari: She whose spirit soars.
587. Dhairya: She who is determination.
588. Turiya: She who is beyond.
589. Vimalatura: She who is the highest expression of purity.
590. Pragalbha: She who is confident.
591. Varunicchaya: She who is the reflection of the cause of equilibrium.
592. Sasini: She who is the radiance of the moon.
593. Visphulingini: She who has subtle radiance.
594. Bhaktih: She who is devotion.
595. Siddhih: She who is perfection.
596. Sadapritih: She who is always beloved.
597. Prakamya: She who is the foremost of all desires.
598. Mahimanima: She who is the mother who is the jewel of the earth.
599. Icchasiddhih: She who is the perfection of all desires.
600. Vasitva: She who is the supreme controller.

601. Isitvordhvanivasini: She who resides above all that is desired.
602. Laghima: She who is extremely small.
603. Gayatri: She who is the wisdom of the three.
604. Savitri: She who is the illuminator of the three.
605. Bhuvanesvari: She who is the supreme ruler of manifested.
606. Manohara: She who takes away thoughts.
607. Cita: She who is consciousness.
608. Divya: She who is divine.
609. Devyudara: She who holds aloft all goddesses.
610. Manorama: She who exemplifies beauty of the mind.
611. Pingala: She who is a subtle avenue by which energy flows.
612. Kapila: She who is like a cow, a giver of pure nourishment.
613. Jihvarasajna: She who has the nectar of wisdom on her tongue.
614. Rasika: She who is all nectar.
615. Rama: She who is beauty.
616. Susumnedayogavati: She who is the spirit of union within the Susumna.
617. Gandhari: She who wears an excellent scent.
618. Narakantaka: She who is the end of all hell.
619. Pancali: She who belongs to the five.
620. Rukmini: She who is the jewel of all circumstances.
621. Radha: She who is the beloved of Krsna.
622. Radhya: She who causes consciousness in the subtle body.
623. Bhama: She who is the mother of illumination.

624. Radhika: She who is the beloved of Krsna; she who is the cause of illumination of consciousness in the subtle body.
625. Amrta: She who is the nectar of immortality.
626. Tulasi: She who is the basil plant.
627. Vrnda: She who is the giver of changes.
628. Kaitabhi: She who constricts.
629. Kapatesvari: She who is the supreme ruler of all fraudulent beings.
630. Ugracandesvari: She who is the ruler of fearful passion.
631. Virajanani: She who is the mother of all heroes and warriors.
632. Virasundari: She who is the beautiful of all warriors.
633. UgraTara: She whose illumination is fearful.
634. Yasodakhya: She who is the light in the eyes of Yasoda.
635. Devaki: She who is the mother of Krsna; she who caused divinity to manifest.
636. Devamanita: She who is obeyed by the gods.
637. Niramjana Cite: She who is formless consciousness.
638. Devi: She who is the goddess.
639. Krodhini: She who is angry.
640. Kuladipika: She who is the light of excellence.
641. Kulavagisvari: She who is the supreme ruler of vibrations.
642. Jvala: She who radiates.
643. Matrka: She who is the mother in the form of letters.
644. Dravani: She who manifests what you value.
645. Drava: She who is what you value.
646. Yogesvari: She who is the supreme ruler of union.

647. Mahamari: She who is the great destroyer.
648. Bhramari: She who comes in the form of a bee.
649. Bindurupini: She who is the intrinsic nature of the form of knowledge.
650. Duti: She who is an ambassador.
651. Pranesvari: She who is the supreme ruler of life.
652. Gupta: She who is hidden.
653. Bahula: She who is everywhere.
654. Damari: She who plays the damaru drum.
655. Prabha: She who is radiant light.
656. Kubjika: She who is hunchbacked or crippled.
657. Jnanini: She who manifests wisdom.
658. Jyestha: She who is oldest.
659. Bhusundi: She who holds the sling.
660. Prakatakrtih: She who manifests without doing.
661. Dravini: She who manifests wealth.
662. Gopini: She who is secretive.
663. Maya: She who is the supreme measurement of consciousness.
664. Kamabijesvari: She who is the supreme ruler of the seed of desire.
665. Priya: She who is the beloved.
666. Sakambhari: She who nourishes with vegetables.
667. Kukanada: She who engenders the seed.
668. Susila: She who is consistently excellent.
669. Tilottama: She who is excellently pure.

670. Ameyavikramakrura: She who manifests unsurpassed grace.
671. Sampacchilativikrama: She who is spinning in the attachment for the loss of wealth.
672. Svastihavyavaha: She who is the conveyance for the offerings of blessings.
673. Priti: She who is the beloved.
674. Usma: She who is the mother of circumstances.
675. Dhumrarcirangada: She who makes the body free from sin.
676. Tapini: She who is heat and light.
677. Tapini: She who is the cause of heat and light.
678. Visva: She who is the universe.
679. Bhogada: She who is the giver of enjoyment.
680. Bhogadharini: She who is the supporter of enjoyment.
681. Trikhanda: She who has three parts.
682. Bodhini: She who manifests wisdom.
683. Vasya: She who is controlled.
684. Sakala: She who is all.
685. Visvarupini: She who is the intrinsic nature of the universe.
686. Bijarupa: She who is the form of the seed.
687. Mahamudra: She who is the great configuration of the cosmos.
688. Vasini: She who controls.
689. Yogarupini: She who is the intrinsic nature of union.
690. Anangakusuma: She who is the flower of infinity.

691. Anangamekhala: She who wears the girdle of infinity.
692. Anangarupini: She who is the intrinsic nature of infinity.
693. Anangamadana: She who is the intoxication of infinity.
694. Anangarekha: She who is the limit of infinity.
695. Anangankusesvari: She who is the supreme ruler of the goad of infinity.
696. Anangamalini: She who is the gardener who cultivated infinity.
697. Kamesvari: She who is the supreme ruler of all desires.
698. Sarvarthasadhika: She who performs discipline for all objectives.
699. Sarvatamtramayi: She who is the the expression of all applications of Spiritual Knowledge.
700. Modinyarunanangarupini: She is the intrinsic nature of the intoxicating light of infinite love.
701. Vajresvari: She is the supreme ruler of lightning.
702. Janani: She is the mother.
703. Sarvaduhkhaksayamkari: She dissolves all pain into the infinite.
704. Sadangayuvati: She is a young lady with six limbs.
705. Yogayukta: She is united in union.
706. Jvalamsumalini: She is the cultivator of radiance.
707. Durasaya: She resides in the distance.
708. Duradharsa: She is a difficult ideal to attain.
709. Durjneya: She gives knowledge that is difficult to attain.
710. Durgarupini: She is the intrinsic nature of the reliever of difficulties.
711. Duranta: She is the end of distance.

712. Duskrtihara: She takes away evil action.
713. Durdhyeya: She is knowledge that is difficult to attain.
714. Duratikrama: She is the mother of all difficult action.
715. Hamsesvari: She is the supreme ruler of laughter.
716. Trikonastha: She resides in a triangle.
717. Sakambharyanukampini: She is the feeling of nourishment from vegetables and produce of the earth.
718. Trijonamilaya: She resides beyond the triangle.
719. Nitya: She is eternal.
720. Paramamrtaramjita: She is the enjoyment of the supreme nectar of immortality.
721. Mahavidyesvari: She is the supreme ruler of the great knowledge.
722. Sveta: She is white or pure.
723. Bherunda: She is formidable.
724. Kulasundari: She is the beauty of excellence.
725. Tvarita: She is quick.
726. Bhaktisamyukta: She is completely united in devotion.
727. Bhativasya: She is under the control of devotion.
728. Santani: She is eternal.
729. Bhaktanandamayi: She is the manifestation of the bliss of devotion.
730. Bhaktabhavita: She is the attitude of devotion.
731. Bhaktasankari: She is the cause of the peace of devotion.
732. Sarvasundaryanilaya: She is the repository of all beauty.
733. Sarvasaubhagyasalini: She is the repository of all good fortune.

734. Sarvasambhogabhavani: She is the mother of all enjoyment.
735. Sarvasaukhyanurupini: She is the intrinsic nature of the feeling of all comforts.
736. Kumaripujanarata: She enjoys the worship of the ever pure one.
737. Kumarivratacarini: She continues the performance of the vow of worship for the ever pure one.
738. Kumari: She is the ever pure one.
739. Bhaktisukhini: She gives the pleasure of devotion.
740. Kumarirupadharini: She wears the form of the ever pure one.
741. Kumaripujakaprita: She loves the worship of the ever pure one.
742. Kumaripritidapriya: She is the beloved of the beloved of the ever pure one.
743. Kumarisevakasamga: She is united in the service of the ever pure one.
744. Kumarisevakalaya: She resides within those who serve the ever pure one.
745. Anandabhairavi: She is the bliss beyond all fear.
746. BalaBhairavi: She is the strength beyond all fear.
747. Batubhairavi: She is youth beyond all fear.
748. Smasanabhairavi: She is in the cremation ground where all fears end.
749. Kalabhairavi: She is time beyond all fear.
750. Purabhairavi: She is in the cremation ground where all fear ends.

751. Mahabhairavapatni: She is the spouse of the great one beyond all fears.
752. Paramanandabhairavi: She is the supreme bliss beyond.
753. Suranandabhairavi: She is divine bliss beyond all fear.
754. Unmattanandabhairavi: She is bliss beyond all fear.
755. Muktyanandabhairavi: She is the bliss of liberation beyond all fear.
756. Tarunabhairavi: She is the energy that pulls beyond fear.
757. Jnanandabhairavi: She is the bliss of wisdom beyond all fear.
758. Amrtanandabhairavi: She is the nectar of immortality beyond all fear.
759. Mahabhayamkari: She is greatly fearful.
760. Tivra: She is very swift.
761. Tivravega: She moves very swiftly.
762. Tarasvini: She takes across.
763. Tripura: She is the resident of the three cities.
764. Paramesani: She is the supreme ruler of all.
765. Sundari: She is the beautiful one.
766. Purasundari: She is completely beautiful.
767. Tripuresvari: She is the supreme ruler of the three cities.
768. Pancadasi: She is the fifteen-lettered one.
769. Pancami: She is the fifth.
770. Puravasini: She is the resident of the city.
771. Mahasaptadasi: She is the great seventeen.
772. Sodasi: She is sixteen.
773. Tripuresvari: She is the supreme ruler of the three cities.

774. Mahamkusasvarupa: She is the intrinsic nature of the great goad.
775. Mahacakresvari Tatha: She is the supreme ruler of the great centers of energy.
776. Navacakresvari: She is the supreme ruler of the nine centers.
777. Cakresvari: She is the supreme ruler of the centers of the energy.
778. Tripuramalini: She is the gardener of the three cities.
779. Rajacakresvari: She is the supreme ruler of the kings of all centers of energy.
780. Vira: She is the female hero.
781. Mahatripurasundari: She is the great beautiful one of the three cities.
782. Sindurappurarucira: She is completely delighted with the red spot of vermilion.
783. Srimattripurasundari: She is the respected beautiful one of the three cities.
784. Savangasundari: Her limbs are all beautiful.
785. Rakta: She is passion.
786. Raktavastrottariyaka: She is clothed in red garment.
787. Yava: She is passion.
788. Yavakasinduraraktacandanadharini: She wears vermilion and red sandal paste.
789. Yavayavakasinduraraktacandanarupadhrk: Her youthful countenance is constantly adorned with red vermilion and red sandal paste.
790. Camari: She is inconstant.

791. Vacakutilanirmalasyamakesini: She is spoken of as one who has pure dark wavy hair.
792. Vajramauktikaratnadyakiritamukutojjvala: In her crown, pearls and jewels are shining like lightning.
793. Ratnakundalasamyuktasphuradgandamanorama: She disseminates a beautiful scent and wears a necklace of radiantly shining jewels.
794. Kunjaresvarakumbhotthamuktaranjitanasika: She wears an extremely beautiful nose ring made from the supreme lord of all jewels and pearls.
795. Muktavidrumamanikyaharadhyastanamandala: She wears a necklace of exquisitely beautiful pearls and jewels in the region of her breast.
796. Suryakantendukantadhyasparsamakanthabhusana: Her throat is shining by the ultimate touch of the sun and the moon.
797. Bijapurasphuradbijadantapamktiranuttama: Her fifteen excellent teeth are completely shining with Bija Mantra.
798. Kamakodandakabhugnabhruyugaksipravartini: Her eye in the middle of her forehead disciplines desire.
799. Matangakumbhavaksoja: Her breasts give nourishment to existence.
800. Iasatkokanadeksana: She especially loves the red lotus flower.
801. Manojnasaskulikarna: She knows the entire path from the ear to the mind.
802. Hamsigatividambini: She is the mother of the swan motion.

803. Padmaragamgadadyotaddoscatuskaprakasini: Her lotus-like body is the illuminator of the four Vedas.
804. Nanamaniparisphuryacchuddhakancanakamkana: She wears bracelets shining with various gems and jewels.
805. Nagendradantanirmanavalayancitapanika: Her fingers of her hands bear rings of ivory and other gems.
806. Amguriyakacitramgi: She wears rings on various parts of her body.
807. Vicitraksudraghantika: She holds an unusually small bell.
808. Pattambaraparidhana: She wears shiny silk clothes.
809. Kalamanjiraranjini: She enjoys the tinkling of cymbals to accompany devotional chanting.
810. Karpuragurukasturikumkumadravalepita: She wears unguents of camphor, woodapple, and musk mixed with red paste.
811. Vicitraratnaprthivikalpasakhatalasthita: She is situated on the earth covered with various jewels at the foot of the tree of all fulfillment.
812. Ratnadvipasphuradratnasimhasananivasini: She sits upon a seat of jewels from the purity of the island of jewels.
813. Satcakrabhedanakari: She pierces the six centers of energy.
814. Paramanandarupini: She is the intrinsic nature of the supreme bliss.
815. Sahasradalapadmantascandramandalavartini:
816. Brahmarupasivakrodananasukhavilasini: She resides in the form of supreme divinity, in the anger of Siva, and in various forms of pleasure.

817. Haravisnuvirancindragrahanayakasevita: She is served by Siva, Visnu, Brahma, Indra and the leaders of the planets.
818. Atmayonih: She is the womb of the soul.
819. Brahmayonih: She is the womb of the supreme divinity.
820. Jagadyonih: She is the womb of the perceivable universe.
821. Ayonija: She does not take birth from any womb.
822. Bhagarupa: She is the form of wealth.
823. Bhagasthatri: She resides within wealth.
824. Bhaginibhagadharini: She upholds wealth and is the wealth.
825. Bhagatmika: She is the capacity for the support of wealth.
826. Bhagadhararupini: She is the intrinsic nature of the manifestation of wealth.
827. Bhagasalini: She responds in wealth.
828. Lingabhidhayini: She is a progenitor of the subtle body.
829. Lingapriya: She is the beloved of the subtle body.
830. Linganivasini: She resides within the subtle body.
831. Lingastha: She is situated in the subtle body.
832. Lingini: She is the capacity of the subtle body.
833. Lingarupini: She is the intrinsic nature of the subtle body.
834. Lingasundari: She is the beautiful one in the subtle body.
835. Lingagitimahapritih: She is greatly enamored of the songs of subtlety.
836. Bhagagitirmahasukha: She derived great pleasure from the wealth of songs.
837. Linganamasadananda: She always takes delight in the subtle name.

838. Bhaganamasadaratih: She is always inspired by the name which bears wealth.
839. Bhaganamasadananda: She is always in bliss with the names which bear wealth.
840. Linganamasadaratih: She is always inspired by the names of subtlety.
841. Lingamalakanthabhusa: She, at whose throat shines forth the garland of subtlety.
842. Bhagamalavibhusana: She shines forth with the garland of wealth.
843. Bhagalimgamrtaprita: She is beloved of the subtle nectar of wealth.
844. Bhagalingamrtatmika: She is the capacity of the subtle nectar of wealth to manifest.
845. Bhagalingarcanaprita: She is the beloved of the offering of subtle wealth.
846. Bhagalingasvarupini: She is the intrinsic nature of subtle wealth.
847. Bhagalingasvarupa: She is the essence of subtle wealth.
848. Bhagalingasukhavaha: She is the conveyance of the pleasure of subtle wealth.
849. Svayambhukusumaprita: She is the beloved of the flower which is born of itself.
850. Svayambhukusumarcita: She is the offering of the flower which is born of itself.
851. Svayambhukusumaprana: She is the life force of the flower which is born itself.

852. Svayambhukusumotthita: She raises aloft the flower which is born of itself.
853. Svayambhukusumasnata: She is bathed by the flower which is born of itself.
854. Svayambhupuspatarpita: She is the offering to ancestors of the flowers which are born of itself.
855. Svayambhupuspaghatita: She is the refuge of the flower which is born by itself.
856. Svayambhupushadharini: She upholds or supports the flower which is born of itself.
857. Svayambhupushatilaka: She who wears a tilak made of the flower born of itself.
858. Svayambhupuspavarcita: She who offers the flowers born of itself.
859. Svayambhupuspanirata: She who is absorbed in the essence of the flower born of itself.
860. Svayambhukusumagraha: She who is beyond the worlds of the flower born of itself.
861. Svayambhupuspayajnamga: She who offers in sacrifice to her own self the flower born of itself.
862. Svayambhukusumatmika: She who is the capacity of the soul to manifest the flower born of itself.
863. Svayambhupusparacita: She who is the expression of the flower born by itself.
864. Svayambhukusumapriya: She who is the beloved of the flower born by itself.

865. Svayambhukusumadanalalasonmattamanasa: She whose mind is intoxicated with desire for the flower born by itself.
866. Svayambhukusumanandalaharisnigdhadehini: She whose friendly body experiences waves of bliss from the flower born by itself.
867. Svayambhukusumadhara: She who supports the flower born by itself.
868. Svayambhukusumakula: She who is the family of the flower born by itself.
869. Svayambhupuspanilaya: She who resides in the flower born by itself.
870. Svayambhupuspavasini: She who sits on the flower born by itself.
871. Svayambhukusumasnigdha: She who is the friend of the flower born by itself.
872. Svayambhukusumotsuka: She who is the supreme pleasure of the flower born by itself.
873. Svayambhupuspakarini: She who is the cause of the flower born by itself.
874. Svayambhupspapalika: She who is the protector of the flower born by itself.
875. Svayambhukusumadhyana: She who is the student or meditator on the flower born by itself.
876. Svayambhukusumajnana: She who is the wisdom of the flower born by itself.
877. Svayambhupuspabhogini: She who is the enjoyer of the flower born by itself.

878. Svayambhukusumananda: She who is the bliss of the flower born by itself.

879. Svayambhupuspavarsini: She who causes the rain of the flower born by itself.

880. Svayambhukusumatsaha: She who is the enthusiasm of the flower born by itself.

881. Svayambhupuspapuspini: She who is the flower of the flower born by itself.

882. Svayambhukusumotsamga: She who is always with the flower born by itself.

883. Svayambhukusparupini: She who is the intrinsic nature of the flower born by itself.

884. Svayambhukusumonmada: She who is the intoxication of the flower born by itself.

885. Svayambhupuspasundari: She who is the beauty of the flower born by itself.

886. Svayambhukusumaradhya: She who is delighted by the flower born by itself.

887. Svayambhukusumodbhava: She who gives birth to the flower born by itself.

888. Svayambhukusumavyagra: She who distinguishes the flower born by itself.

889. Svayambhupuspavarnita: She who expresses the flowers born by itself.

890. Svayambhupukakaprajna: She who is the supreme wisdom of worship of that born by itself.

891. Svayambhuhotrmatrka: She who is the mother of the supreme wisdom of sacrificial worship of that born by itself.
892. Svayambhudatrraksitri: She who protects the bestower of that born by itself.
893. Svayambhubhaktabhavika: She who intuitively understands the attitude of devotion of that born by itself.
894. Svayambhukusumaprajna: She who is the wisdom of the flower born by itself.
895. Svayambhupujakapriya: She who is the beloved of the worship of that born by itself.
896. Svayambhuvandakadhara: She who supports the cause of worship of that born by itself.
897. Svayambhunindakantaka: She who is the cause of the end of that born by itself.
898. Svayambhupradasarvasva: She who is the bestower of all that born by itself.
899. Svayambhunindakantaka: She who is the intrinsic nature of the bestower of that born by itself.
900. Svayambhupradasasmera: She who is the remembrance of the bestower of that born by itself.
901. Svayambharddhasaririni: She who is the half body of that born by itself.
902. Sarvakalodbhavaprita: She who is the beloved who gives birth to all time.
903. Sarvakalodbhavatmika: She who has the capacity of the expression of the soul which gives birth to all time.
904. Sarvakalodbhava: She who is the attitude of all time.

905. Sarvakalodbhavodbhava: She who gives birth to time.
906. Kundapuspasadapritih: She who is the beloved of all the flowers in the receptacle.
907. Golapuspasadagatih: She who always moves with the flowers of light.
908. Kundagolodbhavaprita: She who is the beloved of the light in receptacle.
909. Kundagolodbhavatmika: She who has the capacity of the soul to express the light in the receptacle.
910. Sukradhara: She who is the supporter of purity.
911. Sukrarupa: She who is the form of purity.
912. Sukrasindhunivasini: She who resides within the ocean of purity.
913. Sukralaya: She who has indestructible purity.
914. Sukrabhoga: She who is the enjoyer of purity.
915. Sukrapujasadaratih: She who is delighted by worship with purity.
916. Raktasaya: She who rests in passion.
917. Rakrabhoga: She who is the enjoyer of passion.
918. Rakrapujasadaratih: She who is constantly delighted by worship with passion.
919. Rakrapuja: She who is worshipped with passion.
920. Raktahoma: She who is offered sacrificial offerings with passion.
921. Raktastha: She who is situated in passion.
922. Raktavatsala: She who takes refuge in passion.
923. Raktavama: She who is the description of passion.
924. Raktadeha: She who has the body of passion.

925. Raktapujakaputrina: She who is the daughter born from worship with passion.
926. Raktadyuti: She who is the dignity of passion.
927. Raktasprha: She who is the touch of passion.
928. Devi: She who is the goddess.
929. Raktasundari: She who is beautiful passion.
930. Raktabhidheya: She who knows passion.
931. Raktarha: She who is worthy of passion.
932. Raktakandaravandita: She who is celebrated as the passion of the god of love.
933. Maharakta: She who is great passion.
934. Raktabhava: She who exists in passion.
935. Raktasrstividhayini: She who gives the creation of passion.
936. Raktasnata: She who bathes in passion.
937. Raktasikta: She who is soaked in passion.
938. Raktasevtatiraktini: She who becomes extremely passionate with the selfless service of passion.
939. Raktanandakari: She who manifests the bliss of passion.
940. Raktasadanandavidhayini: She who always gives the bliss of passion.
941. Raktasaya: She who rests within passion.
942. Raktapurna: She who gives full, complete, and perfect passion.
943. Raktasevya: She who is served by passion.
944. Manorama: She who is beautiful.
945. Raktapujakasarvasva: She who is worshipped in all with passion.

946. Raktanindakanasini: She who destroys the criticism of passion.
947. Raktatmika: She who has the capacity of the soul of passion.
948. Raktarupa: She who is a form of passion.
949. Raktakarsanakarini: She who is the cause of the attraction of passion.
950. Raktotsaha: She who is the enthusiasm of passion.
951. Raktadhya: She who rides upon passion.
952. Raktapanaparayana: She who drinks with passion.
953. Sonitanandajanani: She who is the mother of the bliss of the female seed of life.
954. Kallolasnigdharupini: She who is the intrinsic nature of attachment to the family.
955. Sadhakantargata Devi: She who is the goddess who goes inside sadhus.
956. Payini: She who is pure nourishment.
957. Papanasini: She who is the destroyer of all sin (confusion).
958. Sadhakanam Sukhakari: She who is the giver of delight to all sadhus.
959. Sadhakarivininasini: She who destroys the impurity of all sadhus.
960. Sadhakanam Hrdisthatri: She who is situated in the heart of all sadhus.
961. Sadhakanandakarini: She who is the cause of the bliss of all sadhus.
962. Sadhakananca Janani: She who is the mother of the bliss of all sadhus.

963. Sadhakapriyakarini: She who is the cause of the love of sadhus.
964. Sadhakapracuranand Sampatti Sukh Dayini: She who gives the wealth of delight and extreme bliss to sadhus.
965. Sukrapujya: She who is worshipped by purity.
966. Sukrahomasantusta: She who is satisfied with sacrificial offerings of purity.
967. Sukravatsala: She who takes refuge in purity.
968. Sukramurtih: She who is the image of purity.
969. Sukradeha: She who is the embodiment of purity.
970. Sukrastha: She who is situated in purity.
971. Sukrapujakaputrini: She who is the daughter of worship with purity.
972. Sukrini: She who is supreme purity.
973. Sukrasamsprha: She who is the complete touch of purity.
974. Sukrasundari: She who is the beauty of purity.
975. Sukrasnata: She who is bathed in purity.
976. Sukrakari: She who is the manifestation of purity.
977. Sukrasevyatisukrini: She who is the supreme purity served by the pure.
978. Mahasukra: She who is the great purity.
979. Sukrabhava: She who is pure existence.
980. Sukravrstividhayini: She who is the giver of the rain of purity.
981. Sukrabhidheya: She who is the supreme wisdom of purity.
982. Sukrarhasukravandakavandita: The pure of the pure consider her as the worshiped of the worshipped.

983. Sukranandakari: She who is the expression of the bliss of purity.
984. Sukrasadanandavidhayini: She who always gives the bliss of purity.
985. Sukrotsava: She who enjoys the festivals of purity.
986. Sadasukrapurna: She who always manifests full, complete, and perfect purity.
987. Sukramanorama: She who is the beauty of purity.
988. Sukrapujakasarvasva: She who is worshipped as the pure in all.
989. Sukranindakanasini: She who is the destroyer of the criticism of purity.
990. Sukratmika: She who has the capacity of the soul of purity.
991. Sukrasampacchukrakarsakarini: She who is the cause of attraction of the wealth of purity.
992. Sarada: She who is the giver of all.
993. Sadhakaprana: She who is the life force of sadhus.
994. Sadhakasaktamanasa: She who disables the divisive thoughts of sadhus.
995. Sadhakottamasarvasvasadhika: She who is the female sadhu of all excellent sadhus.
996. Bhaktavatsala: She who is the refuge of devotees.
997. Sadhakanandasantosa: She who is completely pleased with bliss.
998. Sadhakadhivinasini: She who is the destroyer of all thoughts of sadhus.
999. Atmavidya: She who is the knowledge of the soul.

1000. Brahmavidya: She who is the knowledge of supreme divinity.
1001. Parabrahmmasvarupini: She who is the intrinsic nature of supreme divinity.
1002. Trikutastha: She who is established in three places.
1003. Pamcakuta: She who is established in five places.
1004. Sarvakutasaririni: She who is the embodiment of all places.
1005. Sarvavamayi: She who is the expression of all that can be expressed.
1006. Varnajapamalavidhyini: She who is the giver of the garland of all expressions which can be recited.

_Chapter : 11_

# Mahavidhyas

### *10 Wisdom Beings: A Journey into the Realm of Mahavidhyas*

The Mahavidhyas stand as radiant jewels, each embodying a unique facet of the divine feminine energy. These ten goddesses, revered in Tantra, are not merely deities but manifestations of the cosmic power that governs creation, preservation, and destruction. As we embark on this sacred journey, we are beckoned to explore the profound symbolism, esoteric wisdom, and transformative energies encapsulated within the Mahavidhyas.

The term "Mahavidhya" translates to "Great Wisdom" or "Great Knowledge," and these goddesses are revered for their transcendental insights and potent energies. Rooted in the Tantric tradition, the worship of Mahavidhyas goes beyond ritualistic practices; it is a profound exploration of the self, an ascent towards spiritual enlightenment, and a communion with the divine.

This exploration will delve into the individual essence of each Mahavidhya, unveiling the layers of symbolism, myths, and practices associated with them. From the fierce Kali to the serene Tripura Sundari, each goddess guides aspirants along a unique path of self-discovery and divine realization.

As we unravel the mysteries surrounding the Mahavidhyas, let us approach with humility, reverence, and a thirst for profound knowledge. Through this journey, may we glean insights that illuminate our spiritual path and forge a deep connection with the divine feminine, transcending time and space.

### *Embarking on the Mystical Journey*

We often forget the incredible power that resides within us—powers that mirror the divine itself. It's a mystical journey, a discovery waiting to unfold, yet many of us look for that divine spark outside ourselves. We believe we are not divine, and so, we search for it in places that may never lead us to the truth.

If we come to recognize the divinity within, transformation occurs. It's like finding the missing piece of a puzzle; suddenly, we are no longer just seekers. Instead, we become a living embodiment of the divine. It's a shift in perception that changes everything.

For those still caught in the illusion of separateness, the journey may seem like going in circles. The pursuit of God outside ourselves can be like chasing a mirage. We keep moving, searching, and seeking, unaware that the true essence lies within, waiting to be discovered.

Imagine walking in circles, always hoping to reach the centre but never quite getting there. That's what happens when we look in the wrong direction, seeking divinity externally. The journey becomes an endless loop, and the elusive centre remains just out of reach.

To truly understand the mystical aspect of self-realization, we need to turn inward. It's a journey into our hearts, where we uncover the profound truth that we've been searching for. It's not about a distant God; it's about realizing the divine spark within us. When this happens, we become the centre of our own cosmic dance.

This journey isn't confined to religious doctrines or complex philosophies. It's a personal experience that goes beyond what our minds can comprehend. It's like waking up to a truth that was always there but somehow eluded us.

So, let's abandon the circular path of external pursuit and embrace the inward journey. It's about discovering the divine tapestry intricately woven within our very being. In this self-realization, we find that the power to become something greater has been within us all along.

The journey is a journey of understanding, acceptance, and embracing our own divinity. It's about recognizing that we are more than we thought— that in the silence of our own hearts, we become the stillness where the dance of life converges into a beautiful unity.

The journey to Godhood unfolds through various paths, each bearing a feminine name— Kali, Tara, Tripura Sundari, Bhuvaneshvari, Bhairavi, Chhinnamasta, Dhumavati, Bagalamukhi, Matangi and Kamala. Despite the diversity of names, the ultimate destination remains consistent: the integration of all forms into the oneness of Godhood, a journey that converges with the realization of the Self.

In the grand symphony of divine powers, all manifestations are inherently feminine. These powers emanate from God, who not only possesses but delights in them. The profound truth lies in the recognition that every individual has the capacity to own these divine powers by experientially understanding the essence encapsulated in the statement, "You are God."

However, two veils of ignorance obstruct this realization. The first is the failure to perceive one's true nature as the identity of God. The second is the erroneous assumption of a limited, manly nature, leading to the illusion of multiplicity. In reality, there is only one thing—Consciousness. It is the illuminating force, the Light of lights, shaping the perception of objects such as the sun, moon, stars, and fire.

The illusion of multiplicity arises from the limited ego, a mental construct characterized by eight bonds—pity, doubt, shame, aversion, class, distinction, and norms of behaviour. These bonds, once seen as components of Consciousness itself, lose their power to bind. The realization that Consciousness is the essence of everything dismantles the egoist structure, unveiling one's true nature.

Each path outlines a self-sufficient guide, uniquely equipped to sever the bonds of ego. These paths, through profound insights and practices, dismantle the layers of illusion that cloak the undifferentiated God manifesting in diverse forms.

The goal of these paths is to lead the seeker to the realization that sins are mere illusions, like origami. Recognizing this truth, one becomes sinless, and in this sinless state, karma loses its power to bind. The journey toward God involves shaking off the shackles of bondage and misery caused by attachments.

Choosing not to remain bound is the pivotal step in the journey toward God. God, in turn, responds abundantly to any effort made by the seeker. The seeker's one step toward God is met with God taking ten steps toward the seeker.

God, as the great amplifier, mirrors the choices made by the individual. Offering God happiness, song, dance, and bliss invites a reciprocal embrace of joy. Conversely, presenting miseries and seeking favours may result in reciprocal challenges. The key lies in making wise choices and eliminating personal bondages.

In this dance toward Godhood, whether through meditation, singing, or dancing, the seeker discovers God within. The relationship is symbiotic, for as the individual embraces God, God becomes one with the individual. The wise choice, the effort to eliminate personal bondages, and the offering of happiness become the threads that intertwine with the divine dance. God, in response, removes all remaining shackles, propelling the seeker toward the ultimate realization—you are God, and your choice is His choice too.

## Kali: The Primordial Force - First Among the Mahavidyas

Kali, a powerful and enigmatic deity, represents the dynamic force of action in the spiritual realm. She embodies the electromagnetic energy that extends across the vast expanse of space, transcending boundaries and permeating all existence. In the cosmic dance of creation, preservation, and dissolution, Kali stands as the primordial force that propels the universe forward.

In understanding the essence of Kali, one delves into the concept of radiation—a fundamental means through which particles communicate their existence across space and time. Radiation serves as the medium for one particle to acknowledge the presence of another, creating a web of interactions that influence the material world. It is within these interactions, facilitated by radiation, that the dimension of time unfolds.

The symbolism of Kali's nakedness holds profound significance. Portrayed as a shameless, naked woman, Kali represents the elimination of interactions that give rise to duality. In the metaphor of the bride and groom, the gaze serves as the probing force, and the blush is the reaction—a dance of interaction that encapsulates the fundamental nature of the universe. Kali, by discarding the trappings of modesty, symbolizes the dissolution of these interactions, echoing the concept that lack of interactions equates to death.

Nakedness, in the symbolic language of Kali, signifies that space itself is the divine attire. Space conceals the pulsating energy—the source of transformation that impacts the positioning of matter and gives rise to the construct of time. The eternal Shivalingam, symbolizing time (Kala), is an intricate creation of Kali, the dynamic energy that propels the cosmic dance.

In the visual representation of Kali standing atop Shiva, the symbolism extends further. Shiva, lying motionless beneath Her feet, symbolizes matter at rest, or rest energy. Kali, the active and dynamic force, stands as the catalyst that propels matter into motion. The juxtaposition of Shiva as the passive and Kali as the active underscores the intricate dance of energy and matter, dynamic and static, within the cosmic play.

The divine synergy between Shiva and Kali reveals the cosmic truth—the interdependence of energy and matter, dynamic forces and stillness, in the grand tapestry of existence. Through Kali's dynamic energy, the universe unfolds, revealing the eternal dance of creation and dissolution, where the boundaries between the active and the passive blur into the seamless flow of cosmic energy.

Time, often perceived as a linear force, is here redefined as a product of interactions rather than an absolute entity. It is emphasized that time does not actively transform; rather, interactions give rise to transformations and create the dimension of time in the process.

The fluid nature of time and space is explored, suggesting that through motion, these dimensions can be exchanged, and even the direction of time can be reversed. The rate at which time flows is intricately connected to energy, with more energetic particles experiencing a slower passage of time. Density is introduced as a property linked to an object's proximity in time to the present, illustrating the dynamic relationship between time and material existence.

The narrative transitions to the esoteric concept of materialization, asserting that the ability to move in time, both into the past and future, is the secret behind this phenomenon. This power is attributed to Kali, who is described as the manifestation of Kundalini within the body—the thunderbolt that explodes during the dissolution of the ego, symbolizing the conquering of time.

Kali is depicted as a powerful force that both destroys and creates, with the destruction symbolized by the garland of heads, reminiscent of the cosmic dance of Shiva Tandava—a metaphor for matter-energy exchanges and a cosmic upheaval. The detachment required to witness such destruction is associated with Shiva, who observes with dispassion the stoppage of time.

**Kali: The Primordial Force - First Among the Mahavidyas**

Kali's impartiality is emphasized, as she spares neither saint nor sinner, seeing beyond human limitations of labelling God as purely good or evil. Kali is recognized as the driving force behind the universe—a thought in the mind of God. Her role as the mother of time does not deter her from destroying time itself to grant the taste of Samadhi to her worshipper.

Kali's symbolism goes beyond destruction, depicting her as the greatest creator. The first entails transporting the present into the past, while the second requires manifesting the unmanifest future—Kali's creative component. Her dark hue represents the unrealized future, and her dual-hand poses offer a message of bravery and blessings, highlighting the fleeting aspect of the cosmos and the eternal character of the person.

Kali, embodying raw power, is presented as a dynamic force that encompasses both the death instinct (Thanatos) and irrepressible Eros. She symbolizes the intense desire and the detached aspect of the burial ground, representing the unity of opposites. The separation of Kali and Kala manifests the world, while their union leads to its disappearance.

Kali's worship is described in two forms: Samhara Kali, representing the dissolved state (Nivrithimarga), and Dakshina Kali, representing the manifest state. Samhara Kali grants death and liberation, while Dakshina Kali offers enjoyment in life and liberation in death. Dakshina Kali invites the worshipper to unite with her, transforming into Samhara Kali during this union. The significance of treating Kali as a mother is highlighted, emphasizing the devotion that prevents desires from arising easily.

The mantra associated with Dakshina Kali is presented along with its mental associations. The mantra reflects the overpowering fire of lust, desire to know, and anger and her worship can lead to a permanent realization of Ardha-Narishwara. The connection between Kali and Sundari Upâsanas is emphasized, noting that the worship alternates between Kali during the dark half of the month and Sundari in the bright half, aligning with the nivrithi and pravrithi paths.

The symbolism of Kali as the hooded Kundalini cobra ready to strike at the Ajna center is described, highlighting the transformative potential of Samhara Kali. Kali is depicted as the combined life force in the world, and the practice to arouse Kundalini involves imagining the breath hitting the muladhara centre with Shakti calan mudra. The narrative provides a glimpse into the esoteric aspects of Kali worship, inviting the seeker to explore the depths of consciousness and the union of opposites within this profound spiritual practice.

The role of Dakshina Kali is described as facilitating the movement of Kundalini in the central channel, the Sushumna Canal. This is achieved by embodying her nature through a combination of intense vairagya (detachment) and a strong desire for creativity. Positioned between the extremes of searching fire and deadening cold lies the warm path of the Sun, symbolizing the sublimated sex drive and the Sushumna canal.

According to Sage Vashishtha, Kali Upasana is done at Svadhisthana because she is Kriya Shakti, the power of action. Individuals lose crucial power due to a lack of control over their breathing and brief breath cycles. Improving life energy entails understanding the nature of "rasa" and practicing conscious breathing, mantra connection, and Kundalini movements in the Svadhisthana region. The implications include upward motions and their repercussions, which represent the core of pure Kali Upasana, which can be done alone or with a partner.

Sage Vashishtha further elaborates on the significance of aware breathing, highlighting its "mahima" or greatness. Aware breathing is identified as one of the eight siddhis, conferring control over time, knowledge of the past over the present, empowerment of the mind, speech, and eyes, as well as longevity. Additionally, aware breathing is associated with liberation, signifying the elimination of ego and the corresponding shackles it creates.

The siddhis include vaksuddhi, where whatever one speaks becomes true; control over time, enabling knowledge of past lives and the future, removing the fear of death; power to the mind, allowing deep insights into divine nature; power to the speech, eyes, and long life. Liberation, in this context, implies freedom from the ego, leading to spiritual emancipation. The narrative emphasizes the transformative power of aware breathing in achieving these profound siddhis and spiritual advancements.

Sage Vasishtha describes Kali as "**samvarga vidya**," which translates to the knowledge relating to the mind (where "**sam**" refers to the mind and "**varga**" to relating to or shakti). Kali is also known as "**prana vidya**," and in the Upanishads, it is referred to as "*Udgitha-vidya*." To those who are materialistically oriented, Kali may appear as a sword that strikes them, but for yogis, she is the sword in their hands.

The metaphor of Kali as the sword in the hands of yogis is apt. It suggests that the power she represents can be used both for destruction and creation. This underscores the importance of self-control for yogis, as they must exercise their power responsibly and avoid using it for harmful purposes.

The cautionary note about the siddhis (spiritual powers) associated with such practices, emphasizing their potential danger. Siddhis can be powerful and transformative, but if not approached with wisdom and ethical considerations, they may lead to negative consequences. The reminder to "beware" serves as a warning to practitioners to exercise caution and responsibility in their spiritual journey, especially when dealing with potent forces and abilities.

## Tara: The Guiding Star - Illuminating Wisdom Among the Mahavidyas

Tara, the second path to self-realization, is likened to a star in the dark night bursting forth a sphere of light out of the vacuum—the manifestation of the unmanifest sound of Omkara. Tara holds profound meanings. Firstly, she is Tarini, guiding you beyond, a bridge to immortality, symbolized by Omkara. Secondly, Tara is a high-pitched sound, reflecting the transformation of Omkara from the heart center into supersonic sound, light, and darkness as the frequency descends. Thirdly, Tara is the lover of the Moon, seduced by Brhaspati, the intelligent counsellor to the Gods. This illustrates manifestation as a reduction in bandwidth, a ray of infinite frequency, with Tara worshipped at the physical level for self-realization.

In its highest Vedic meaning, Tara is the mantra OM, the pure sound of Pranava. In the tantric context, Tara is worshipped as Hrim Strim Hum Phat, where the goddess Maya is seduced and dispelled by the fire of Shiva's knowledge. In the Buddhist mantra of Mahayana or Vajrayana sects, Tara takes the form OM Hrim Strim Hum Phat, emphasizing control over physical and mental seduction. The significance of the explosive sound "Phat" lies in its symbolization of piercing darkness with light, leading to a transformative explosion of frequencies, from bodily vibrations to feelings, sound, heat, silence of radio waves, light, and beyond in the meditative journey.

The sensory mechanisms of the body respond only to the shaded zones, disregarding the others. The second branch encompasses regions I, II, and III—Para, Madhyama, and

Pashyanti. When modulated by the throat and tongue into meaningful words, region II is known as Vaikhari. As Kundalini ascends, it traverses Para, Pashyanti, Madhyama, and finally Vaikhari in the sound branch. In the light branch, it transforms through infrared, visible light, ultraviolet, and the invisible spectrum of black, cold light, including x-rays, gamma-rays, and cosmic rays, along with matter waves.

After sound subsides, light emerges, and after light fades, awareness persists in *sunyata*. Contrary to the misconception of sunyata as emptiness, it represents the incomprehensible completeness of variety, profound in knowledge and awareness. Consider the analogy of listening to music. The tempo intensifies, and rhythm accelerates until no rhythm can keep pace, merging into a steady monotone of unmanifest silence—a one-pointed awareness vibrating at an infinite frequency. This state is not the lethargy of sleep but the stillness of a spinning top, illustrating the essence of the difference between Samadhi and sleep.

It should be realized that the combined bandwidth of Para, Pashyanti, and Madhyama is far below that of light waves, and the bandwidth of light waves is far below that of awareness or matter waves, which always move faster than light, thereby moving backwards in time. (Anything moving faster than light must move back in time.) Thus, Buddha's assertion that silence and *Sunyata* are the nature of the universe aligns with the Upanishads, which state that the manifest universe is only the tail of Brahman.

Physics recognizes three types of particles: particles, light waves, and antiparticles. Particles move forward in time, antiparticles move backwards, and light freezes the present. When corresponding particles and antiparticles meet, they explosively annihilate, producing light. Therefore, light results from pair annihilation, while knowledge emerges from the union of past and future in the present. The nature of the present is bliss. Buddhist philosophy advises eliminating desires, rooted in duality, to eradicate misery. In the present moment lies realization, and deviating from it—whether through remembering or planning—means losing contact with the purity, bliss, and nirvana of the present. In reality, there is no past, no future—only an ever-moving present moment containing all of infinite time within it. There is no time away from the present.

Tara is the Pashyanti sound, overlapping Madhyama in frequency. The power of manifest sound serves as a bridge to the God within the human system, and this power is referred to as Om. The symbol "Om" imitates the sound within, and while the external symbol has a beginning and an end, the inner sound is ever-present. Tara, pointed to by the Om symbol, takes various forms. One form, Nila, symbolizes the dark or Tamas nature, unmanifested, and unclearness. Nila is the most pious manifestation, as Om is a unique name for Ishwara. Patanjali emphasizes that Om points to Ishwara, and without hearing Om within, the use of any mantra is futile. The Vedas also state that one who has not heard the Om within has no use for their song.

Om permeates all sounds, enlivening them individually. Vowels carry Om most effectively, with the Vedas containing the highest quality of sound. Protecting the sound of the mantra is crucial. When sages meditate, listening to the sound of Om in their heart, throat, and head centres, waves called mantras arise spontaneously from the ocean of Om. Each mantra has a seer, a Rishi who heard or saw the mantra during meditation. Mantras are natural sound wave flows controlling manifestations of Omkara. By meditating on Om, one can receive mantras from Tārā or Saraswati. Meditating on these mantras results in the transmission of knowledge from that wave, forming the content of the mantra. Mantras arise without effort during meditation, and they design and create themselves. Mantras are living sounds, possessing life, and only the unlimited intellect of God can build life from a genetic code. A mantra is the genetic code of a deity, and by repeating this code, a human is made. Mantras manifest God through repetition, resulting in various forms such as joy, peace, power, dance, art, poetry, prose, Vedas, Puranas, Agamas, Nigamas, and more. Vedas, containing the highest light and wisdom, provide the mostly true and accurate depiction of godliness, as does the religious text of every religion.

Absolute truth cannot be conveyed in words, and all words are mere mappings of the truth, containing some degree of lie by necessity. It is a matter of how much truth is present. The truth here refers to the resemblance of the idea formed in the reader to the idea that prompted the seer or writer. In most cases, the resemblance is sadly lacking.

Vedas are direct revelations, as are the revelations of seers and jnanis in their meditation (dhyana). They all have the same validity, containing the highest degree of resemblance to the reality seen. They are called Shukla, the white, or the manifest Tārā.

Whenever the ego breaks free from the body—whether in sleep, coitus, death, or Samadhi—profound joy is experienced. Sleep and death share similarities, as do coitus and Samadhi, with the only difference being the timescales involved. Orgasm and Samadhi also differ primarily in timescales, where death is a continuous sleep, and Samadhi is a continuous orgasm. In both cases, one transcends the ego, experiencing a blissful state.

The sage in the continuous splendour of Samadhi faces a dilemma: not wanting to emerge from such blissful states, resulting in union with God or Yoga. Ordinary coitus becomes an imitation, a passing recollection of the infinite divine ecstasy called Brahmananda, represented by Ardhanareesvara Tattva.

Vedic knowledge and proper meditation can lead to infinite joy through the study and practice of Vedas, Upanishads, Agamas, and Nigamas. Agamas, originating from Shiva's head and entering Girija's face, emphasize worshipping the genitals as the first step toward sublimation. In Hindu and Vajrayana pantheism, the erotic element plays a vital role, present in all temples. Eros was worshipped by householders, and Kama had a significant place in society, elevated to an art form known as Sringara.

The study of Vedas, Upanishads, Agamas, and Nigamas provides the worship of Saraswati, the creative power of Brahman, called Sukla Upasana. Nila Upasana involves studying the source of revelations to obtain them personally. Tara Upasana is the third form, called Citra, where one practices constant awareness of unmanifest sound within, researching the sound of the mantra to reveal unmanifest sound. Tara is Aksara Vidya in the Upanishads, representing the transcendence upwards through Udgitha Vidya.

Upasana with mantras involves reciting Om alone, leading to the Yoga path. Mantras like Om Hrim Strim Hum Phat, Hrim Strim Hum Phat, Hrim Strim Hum can be practiced by Parasakti and Parama purusha, eliminating illusions of others. In Tara Upasana, if the physical union is used, it must be with para sakti, not sva sakti, as ejaculation is forbidden. Both Hindu and Buddhist unions meet in Tara, insisting on parashakti and forbidding male ejaculation. In Sundari Upasana, all males and females are considered Sivas and Saktis, aspiring for Yoga.

Para sakti becomes necessary to break down the walls of identification with one's partner, and further, to break down the notion of the other. The ultimate goal is group identity in Tripura Sundari, where identities of all Gods and Goddesses are established within one's body. Sundari represents the final act, bringing physical bliss through the mating of Gods and Goddesses, depicted as a circle in Srichakra. In the study of Tara Tantra, Para sakti is essential, envisaging both group identity and withdrawal (nivritti) in the form of Nigama Upasana, creating a blissful union. Citra Upasana involves observing sounds without turning away from the unpleasant or seeking the pleasant, being a detached observer.

Speaking the truth, studying well, and remembering teachings are essential in Sukla Upasana. In Citra Upasana, one observes sounds in others' voices without turning away from the unpleasant. Sarasvati is the bliss of speaking from the tip of the tongue, representing orgasmic union and creativity with detachment. Sanyasa is an outgrowth of Yoga, where lower pleasures are not spurned but intelligently used to break down ego barriers and reach Samadhi.

Tara Tantra, through the study and practice of Vedas, Upanishads, Agamas, and Nigamas, offers a path of worshipping Saraswati, personal revelations, and constant awareness of unmanifest sound. This comprehensive approach encompasses Para sakti, bringing together Hindu and Buddhist principles, and concludes in the blissful circle of Sundari Upasana, where all initiates are considered Sivas and Saktis, aspiring for Yoga.

# Tripura Sundari:
# The Radiant Beauty and Divine Sovereignty Among the Mahavidyas

Sundari or Tripurasundari embodies the essence of consciousness—a graceful, harmonious, joyous, and powerful manifestation symbolized by the lotus of lotuses. She is The Most Beautiful, bringing forth divine knowledge and love. As Adishakti, the mother of mothers, she emanates as Lakshmi, Saraswati, and Gowri. These three goddesses represent different aspects of the Adishakti, revealing the upward thrust of evolution not only for individual liberation but for the entire class of classless human beings. In Tibetan mandalas of Vajrayana Buddhism, Sundari is a significant presence, playing with elements like the moon, rainbows, space, and the sun. Her symbolic representation in OM as Three Pura Sundari reflects her role in all three aspects of creation—nourishment and destruction.

Sundari is the primal power of God, Adishakti, expressing the divine's desire to manifest itself in various forms. Her existence is rooted in the first desire, known as Kamakala or Ichcha Shakti. Desire, the secret of creation, is the driving force behind manifestation and the sustenance of existence. The desire unfolds as a division in the Supreme Being, seeking unity in all fragmented parts. The Divine desires to sacrifice itself in creation and subsequently desires to reintegrate the creation into itself. This two-fold desire forms the basis of Love—an enduring bond that connects the creator and the created. Sundari is identified with Hrim, the combination of Hari(Vishnu), Hara(Shiva), and Virinchi(Brahma). She is

Vishnu Maya, the great illusion, continuously assuming new forms and exuding procreative bliss.

Sundari is described in 108 letters in the three Vedas, symbolizing the union of Shiva and Shakti, the primal power. The Gayatri mantra is decoded to reveal the corresponding Sri Vidya mantra of fifteen letters. These letters are categorized into three parts—Vagbhava kuta, representing willpower generation, and Shakti kuta, symbolizing the divine union between Saraswati with Brahma, Lakshmi with Vishnu, and Gowri with Shiva.

### *Vagbhava kuta, focusing on the first part of the Pancadasi mantra:*

'Tat Savitur Varenyam' corresponds to the letters 'ka' and 'e.' 'Tat' represents Brahma, the permanent, attributeless, and blemishless creator. 'Savitur Varenyam' denotes the divine yoni, the central and enjoyable part of creative power, represented by the letter 'e.' This letter encapsulates the essence of Savitur Varenyam and is worshipped as the live giver. The sexual symbolism is multi-layered, encompassing the physical, mental, and spiritual levels, emphasizing the importance of Consciousness, desire, and action arising from interactions.

The symbolism of Sundari and the decoding of the mantra reflect the profound spiritual teachings, emphasizing the interconnectedness of desire, love, and the eternal dance of creation and dissolution.

Bhargo Devasya Dhi: Bhargo Deva represents Shiva's nature of continuous abhishekam, and anointing. The continuous flow of awareness from head to foot, called amrita snanam, cools the 72,000 nerves(energy points) in the body, purifying them from accumulated sins, karmas, and bondages. 'Dhi' signifies the earth, illustrating ultimate dharana—a rock-like steadiness of thought flow. The earth, by its stillness, demonstrates the highest form of concentration. 'La' is a symbol for the earth and is most appropriate for Shiva, signifying indestructible potency for creative orgasmic bliss while maintaining form. In Buddhist terms, this indestructibility is known as Vajra, representing egoless bliss.

Dhiyoyonah Prachodayat: This phrase alludes once again to silence. It signifies the movement of rock-like steady awareness from rajas into sattva. Pure sattva is characteristic of Vishnu. The symbol for this process is 'Hrim,' with shyness being its essential component—shyness in expressing love but desiring it ardently.

### *This is the Kamaraja Kuta, unveiled by Tripura Sundari as Lakshmi to her Lord, Vishnu:*

Paro Rajase Savadhom - May the rock-like steady flow of awareness move beyond rajas into sattva. Pure sattva is characteristic of Vishnu. The Gopis, representing jeevas, are irresistibly drawn by the love of the Lord, dancing to the tune of Krishna's Murali. Krishna's flute symbolizes the Anahatha in one's own heart, drawing the jeeva to the Lord. 'Ha' is Shiva (outgoing breath), 'Sa' is Shakti (incoming breath), and the bindu between them results from their union, representing kumbhaka. The Bindu is a symbol for the mixing of male and female genital fluids, kumbhaka, and the mind. It signifies the union of jeeva with Paramatman, universal egoless love on a cosmic scale is attained by concentrating on the heart center. The heart center is where one hears the call of Krishna. Krishna, in the female form, is Lalita, satisfying all the desires of Her devotees. The integration of jeeva with Paramatman is complete when one realizes the bisexuality within oneself, expressing the opposite partner (kundalini) within. Having experienced the highest union, one no longer craves physical union, as its ability to satisfy is inferior, and it entails the cost of bondage. Desires naturally dissipate because, in a state of oneness with God, there is no gap between desire and fulfillment.

### *Shakti Kuta, symbolizing time (Kala) in union with his Samhara Shakti, Kali:*

Tat Savitur Varenyam: From the best part of creativity, space is created, followed by air, the remaining three great elements, the mind, and the ego (jeeva). Jeeva, the best part of the creative chain, deserves the light of the sun, the union with the divine at all levels. 'Sa' represents the illuminating consciousness.

The intimate relationship between life and death is emphasized. Death, symbolized by the hooded cobra, observes the light of life between the eyebrows. Light is seen when a photon dies in the retina, giving rise to the consciousness of light. The continuous pleasure of seeing light results from the continuous death of photons, and this mirrors the role of Shiva as the Lord of death. Life and death are inseparable—something must continuously die to allow life to exist. Shiva as Kala must die continuously so that a new time can be born. Without death, there can be no life, and vice versa. Life is Tripura Sundari (Kali), and death is Shiva. The source of life is death, and the source of death is life. Both sides of the coin are inseparable, representing the profound dance between life and death.

# Bhuvaneshwari: The Divine Mother of the Universe Among the Mahavidyas

Bhuvaneshwari is the embodiment of integrating and unifying knowledge, serving as the genesis of the seven worlds both above and below. Her essence lies in the profound act of seeing, which is synonymous with perception. Often referred to as Maya or Shuddha Vidya, Bhuvaneshwari explores the multifaceted origins of knowledge.

In the realm of knowledge, two primary sources exist. The first emanates from sensory perception, constituting the foundational origin of knowledge. The second class encompasses knowledge derived from devices that enable seeing, reliving past experiences, and projecting desires. This knowledge is divided into memory-driven projections and revelations occurring in seedless meditations.

Bhuvaneshwari's worship aims to foster a direct experiential understanding of God. It challenges the notion of artificially imposed restrictions on individual consciousness, advocating for transcending these limitations through unconventional means.

Shambhavi Mudra: The practice involves a unique mode of seeing where the eyes are intentionally defocused, allowing one to perceive the space between or beyond objects. This unconventional method disrupts the habitual act of focusing on an object, unveiling the illusory nature of the world and revealing its true essence.

Open-Eyed Meditation: Bhuvaneshwari's open-eyed meditation through Shambhavi Mudra offers a transformative experience. By defocusing the eyes, practitioners can transcend the multiplicity of the world into a singular, unified perception.

The method may pose challenges when applied to everyday objects due to ingrained focusing habits and emotional associations. Therefore, starting with objectless spaces like the sky is recommended for ease of practice.

Bhuvaneshwari as Jnana Shakti symbolizes perceptive power leading to knowledge, embodying Jnana Shakti. She represents the space concept in creation, the ethereal medium through which light extends. Space, as an extension of perception, mirrors the range of vision. Bhuvaneshwari, through her all-pervasive force, creates, sustains, and nourishes the primordial worlds.

Māyā: Also known as Māyā, Bhuvaneshwari reflects the infinite consciousness with the power to manifest in finite forms. Māyā, often interpreted as an illusion, is viewed by tantric as the divine's ability to clothe itself in varied, finite expressions. The measured-out space, the perception of the Divine, and the force of the first knowledge reside in Bhuvaneshwari.

Mantra - Hrim: The sacred mantra 'Hrim,' denoting illusion, serves as a constant reminder to avoid falling into the illusions of focus and detail. Instead, it encourages practitioners to perceive beyond these aspects, recognizing the unifying identity underlying all.

Tantric Pranava - Om Hrim Om: In some practices, the mantra is expanded to 'Om Hrim Om,' emphasizing the connection between the space within one's heart and the infinite space outside. Hrim, recognized as the tantric Pranava, signifies the sound of Space, expressing a yearning cry from the created towards the Creator.

Hrim also referred to as the 'lajjā beeja,' implies a manifestation not yet fully blossomed, capturing the ongoing evolution of the worlds created by Bhuvaneshwari. It represents the sound of Space itself—a yearning cry echoing the desire of the created to connect with the vast immensities.

Her worship leads practitioners to an identity view, where they perceive themselves everywhere initially. As this spiritual journey unfolds, external world observations gradually diminish, and individuals find themselves consistently merged in the oneness of God, fostering profound self-love.

Bhuvaneshwari holds a pivotal position in the pantheon of Shakti worshippers, appearing threefold in Pancadasi as Sarasvati, Lakshmi, and Gauri.

# Bhairavi:
# The Fierce and Formidable
# Aspect of the Supreme Goddess

Bhairavi, also known as Ananda Bhairavi or Tripura Bhairavi, transcends mere definition. She is the fifth essence, a melodic raga with ascendant and descendant notes that dance in the mystical realms of sound. In the realm of musical aesthetics, she emerges as a **vakra raga** *(ragas that have swaras arranged in a zig-zag manner)*, a composition where the ascending and descending notes weave a unique tapestry.

Experience Bhairavi as para, a term shrouded in enigma, leading seekers to the realms of awareness, existence, and bliss. In the embrace of Bhairavi, one encounters the divine sparsha devata, the goddess who revels in contact—a celestial dance of intimate connection.

Much like Sundari, who resides in the three paras, Bhairavi mirrors this cosmic triad, distinguished only by the nuanced spectrum of sound frequencies one chooses to embrace. Bhairavi, with her low-frequency vibrations, awakens currents that are not merely heard but felt—a tidal ebb and flow resonating in the depths, particularly in the sacred Muladhara chakra.

In the symphony of spiritual practices, where Kali's worship embodies anger, and Sundari's dance weaves between knowledge, affection and action, Bhairavi stands singular. Her focus is singular, her centre is Muladhara, and her mood is the sublime ecstasy of enjoyment—***ananda***, the rasa of union.

## The Art of Defocusing Reality

Sambhavi Mudra, the key to Bhairavi's open-eyed meditation, invites practitioners to defy the conventional norms of perception. It challenges the habitual act of focusing on external objects and instead encourages the intentional defocusing of the eyes. Through this unconventional lens, one gazes not at the object but at the projection from the universal mind on the object—an avenue where the illusory nature of the world dissolves, revealing the truth that lies beneath the surface.

## Bhairavi's Kundalini Power: The Roar of Unremitting Bliss

Bhairavi personifies the surging, raging power of Kundalini—a maddeningly deep joy unbridled by the tranquility of calmness. The Muladhara, the focal point of Bhairavi's upasana, becomes the epicenter where Kundalini roars like a caged lion. Here, she manifests as unremitting sexual bliss, a relentless force that seeks to transcend the confines of the physical and embrace the divine union.

The sacred mantra 'Hsraim Hsklrim Hsrsauh' unveils the divine symphony of Bhairavi. Each syllable bears profound significance— 'H' for Siva, 'S' for Sakti, and 'R' representing the fire of desire that yearns for the union between the two. This fiery mantra echoes the lusty mating that transpires in the citkala of Bhairavi upasana.

## The Divine Revelation: Jata Vedase Sunavame Soma Arati Yato Nidahati Vedah:

The revelation of Bhairavi emanates from the Vedic mantra 'Jata Vedase Sunavame Soma Arati Yato Nidahati Vedah.'

Within these verses, she unfolds as Saraswati, intoxicated with knowledge yet desiring prolific creation in her tamasic form. This synthesis of *saguna* and *nirguna*, the divine and formless, encapsulates the essence of Liberation.

Bhairavi's Liberating Embrace: Svaha and Svadha

Bhairavi, in her boundless perception, recognizes no distinctions. Every man becomes her husband and lover. She becomes the devourer of sins, consuming them in the fire of her knowledge, personifying 'Svaha.' Simultaneously, she revels in the pleasures of the divine realms, earning the name 'Svadha.' The profound meaning of 'Svaha' unfolds as 's' for Sakti, 'va' for amritam, and 'ha' for Shiva—a sacred offering symbolizing the generation of divine nectar through the union of purusha and stri.

## *Tantric Liturgy: Journeying through Orgastic Worship*

The tantric liturgy of Tripura Bhairavi, as detailed in Sarada Tilakam, Mantra Mahodadhi, and various tantric texts, delves into the ecstatic worship of this divine goddess. The moaning mantras in Jayadi-homa reveal the high value placed on heavenly pleasures in Vedic society, transcending the limitations of human morals.

## *The Art of Pleasure in Heaven: Gandharva Vivaha*

Bhairavi upasana introduces Gandharva Vivaha as a valid means for unrestricted enjoyment and liberation. The Vedic mantras of marriage, with their hidden meanings, unveil the nature of pleasures in heaven, where divine professionals engage in pious and liberated acts beyond human constraints.

### *Tripura Upanishad: An Illuminated Path to Oneness*

The Tripura Upanishad, a beacon of wisdom, unfolds the path to oneness. The pursuit of Sundari and Bhairavi upasana reveals the intimate connection between identity and the divine. The Satakshari Vidya of Tripuratapini Upanishad unveils the interconnectedness of the three goddesses—Sundari, Bhairavi, and Pracandacandika—leading aspirants toward immortality.

In the culmination of Tripura Upanishad, the sacred mantra 'Om Hrirn Om Hrim' emerges as a symbolic expression of the profound interaction between purusha and prakriti. It encapsulates the fiery dance of desire and the divine, marking the sacred end to the journey through Bhairavi's realm.

In the cosmic dance orchestrated by Bhairavi, the seeker finds not only the symphony of sound but the unraveling of the self—a journey that transcends inhibitions, embracing the completeness of existence, and culminating in the blissful liberation of the soul.

# Chinnamasta:
# The Fierce Illumination of Lightning and Thunder

In the cosmic dance of creation, where Prakriti and the seed of God intertwine, Chinnamasta emerges as a manifestation of awe-inspiring force and violent beauty. She stands amidst the elements—flash, thunder, rain, rivers, green fields, flowers, and fruits—where life thrives in the eternal embrace of Mother Earth, and the vision of God takes root.

## *The Divine Sacrifice: Severing and Sustaining*

Chinnamasta, the headless goddess, orchestrates a profound sacrifice—the flash that separates the head from the body, and three streams of blood burst forth. In this enigmatic dance, the central stream is consumed by the severed head she holds, while the remaining two streams nourish her attendants. This act symbolizes the eternal cycle of creation, destruction, and sustenance.

Standing stark naked, robed in dazzling light, Chinnamasta's nudity, though evident, is veiled by the radiance that envelops her. Headless yet sublime, she stands in maithuna on Rati and Manmatha, embodying the transformative power of sexual energy. The goddess's sacrifice offers kapāla moksha, a liberation beyond death itself.

## *Prakâsha and NAda: Precursors of Creation*

In the metaphysical realms of creation, the interplay of Prakâsha (Light) and NAda (Sound) catalyzes Chinnamasta's emergence. Prakâsha, when delimited as Âkâsha, becomes Buhvaneshwari; delimitation as Time forms KAli.

Chinnamasta embodies the transcendent aspect of Prakâsha, involved in creation yet transcending it—an embodiment of the unmanifest Sound in concentrated consciousness.

### *Chinnamasta: The Self-Decapitated Goddess of Transformation*

Chinnamasta arises from the forceful interaction of Prakâsha and NAda, resulting in a violent creation almost severed from its source. This cosmic purpose, a divinely orchestrated delight in separate existences, manifests as Chinnamasta severing the head—the very source of creation.

In the tangible world, the interaction of Light and Sound manifests as thunder and lightning. Chinnamasta, the thunder, annihilates anti-divine forces, hidden within the heart of the cloud's radiance. As the ruler of the cosmic mind, she guides the human mind, acting as the unseen force behind the senses. Symbolically trampling Rati and Manmatha, joined in amorous union, Chinnamasta offers mastery over the sex impulse—a pathway to profound worship.

## Prachanda Chandika: The Unyielding Force

Chinnamasta's action, more formidable than the fierce KAli, earns her the name Prachanda Chandika. While KAli works through the aid of Time (KAla), Chinnamasta, representing electric force (vidyut shakti), destroys instantaneously. Seated between the eyebrows (ajna chakra), she commands the power of will and vision.

### *Lightning Energy and the Sushumna: Cosmic Connection*

Chinnamasta, the embodiment of lightning energy (Vajra Vairochani), spreads herself through myriad channels, enveloping the cosmos. As beings are created, this energy enters through the Bramharandhra, connecting the body's energy flow with that of the cosmos. Sushumna, the central nâdi, becomes the conduit for this energy, and Chinnamasta resides in concentrated form at the ajna chakra.

### *The Sustaining Current: Chinnamasta's Cosmic Flow*

In the Sushumna, Chinnamasta traverses as the sustaining current of electric energy, limited only by the granthis or knots. These knots, symbolic of obstacles, are severed by the scissors in her hand. Prachanda Chandika is the current coursing through Sushumna, while Varini and DAkini represent currents through Ida and Pingala.

### *The Mother of Parashurâma: Symbolism in Creation*

Chinnamasta, manifested as the mother of Parashurâma, symbolizes the cosmic play of creation and sacrifice. The story, where Parashurâma, in unquestioning obedience, severs his mother's head and later revives her, portrays the cyclical nature of life, death, and rebirth.

### *The Dhenu Beeja: Mastery over the Senses*

Chinnamasta's sacred mantra, the seed-sound 'Hum' or Dhenu beeja, grants mastery over the senses and annihilates the mind. To engage in effective sadhana, practitioners immerse themselves in the visualization of a constant downpour of lightning, submitting the entire being to the divine force with absolute dedication and surrender.

### *Chinnamasta: The Resplendent Dance of Creation*

In the sublime ballet of cosmic creation, where the ethereal meets the earthly, Chinnamasta emerges—a tapestry woven with flashes of light, echoes of thunder, the nurturing touch of rain, and the verdant expanse of green fields adorned with blossoms and fruits. Here, life takes root in the eternal bosom of Mother Earth, awakening the divine vision within.

### *The Divine Enigma: A Sacrifice of Radiance*

Chinnamasta, the headless goddess, orchestrates a celestial sacrifice—a flash that separates the divine head from its earthly vessel. Three rivulets of life-giving blood cascade forth, unveiling a sacred spectacle. The central stream, an elixir of vitality, is consumed by the divine head she holds aloft, while her devoted attendants partake in the remaining two, weaving a cosmic dance of sustenance and transformation.

### *Stark Beauty in Radiant Robes*

Standing in the sacred act of maithuna, stark naked yet veiled in the brilliance of illuminating light, Chinnamasta embodies both vulnerability and divinity. Her nudity, rather than a mere physicality, becomes a celestial garment—an ethereal robe shimmering with the brilliance that transcends the gaze.

The Thunder of Cosmic Forces, Chinnamasta, the indomitable force, personifies the thunderous power of the Supreme. Beyond the fierceness of Kali, she earns the title of Prachanda Chandika—an embodiment of untamed strength. Her actions transcend the fierce and terrible, bestowing an instantaneous destruction that echoes through the cosmos.

In the prelude to creation, Prakasha and Nada converge in a divine symphony. Prakasha, when shaped as Akasha, becomes Buhvaneshwari; its dance with Time births Kali. In this cosmic symphony, Chinnamasta emerges as the precipitate—a forceful interaction of light and sound that nearly severs creation from its divine source.

In the ethereal realm, Chinnamasta traverses as a concentrated force at the ajna chakra. Here, in the cosmic dance, she weaves herself along myriad channels, enveloping the cosmos in a radiant embrace. Through Bramharandhram, the cosmic energy flows, binding the universe with the sacred thread of creation.

Chinnamasta, the embodiment of Vajra Vairochani, becomes the sustaining current through the cosmic river of Sushumna. A relentless force, she traverses the divine conduit, limited only by the knots symbolizing obstacles. With scissors in hand, she severs these knots, becoming the dynamic force coursing through the ethereal channels.In the dance of Chinnamasta, the cosmic ballet reveals itself—a symphony of sacrifice, creation, and the eternal renewal of life's sacred dance.

# Dhumâvati:
# The Enigmatic Veil of Cosmic Slumber

In the genesis of existence, where darkness conceals itself within darkness, and the vast expanse is draped in Non-Being, emerges the profound declaration: "From the Non-Being, the Being was born. Into the Non-Being shall the Being dissolve again." Thus, the cosmic tapestry weaves itself, with Dhumâvati reigning over the primal state— the cradle of creation's inception and the sanctuary of its eventual withdrawal.

## *The Divine Widow: Goddess of Inconscience*

Dhumâvati, adorned in the poignant narrative of cosmic cycles, stands as the solitary widow goddess, the harbinger of conscience. Having orchestrated the slumber of her husband, she governs the interplay between existence and non-existence—a celestial dance where the potentiality of Being rests within the womb of Non-Being.

## *The Portrait of Ugliness: A Divine Paradox*

In the sacred canvas of symbolism, Dhumâvati emerges, a paradoxical embodiment of distortion and perversion. Her countenance, pale and veiled in smoky hues, transcends conventional notions of beauty. Long limbs, sparse teeth, sagging breasts—these physical attributes become an artistic reflection of the cosmic disarray she personifies. Draped in uncouth attire with disheveled hair, she commands attention from her chariot, bearing a raven banner, symbolizing the dark wisdom she imparts.

### *From Darkness to Smoky Light: The Alchemy of Existence*

While Dhumâvati dwells in the shadows of non-being, her smoky hue carries within it the embryonic essence of light. The darkness she embodies is not absolute; rather, it intertwines with the latent warmth of a hidden flame. In this alchemical dance between Being and Non-Being, the Goddess becomes the living bridge between the contrasting states of reality.

### *Yoga Nidra: Dhumâvati's Cosmic Siesta*

As the Maha yoga nidra of Vishnu, Dhumâvati symbolizes the cosmic slumber that envelops the all-pervading primordial principle. From his infinite couch, amidst the milky ocean of bliss, Vishnu withdraws into yoga nidra—a profound sleep that foretells an imminent awakening, a precursor to the divine projection of Godhead. Dhumâvati, in this cosmic rest, becomes the fertile womb of unmanifested worlds awaiting rebirth.

### *The Annihilation of Enemies: A Sacred Offering*

In the worship of Dhumâvati, the celestial battlefield unfolds. She, the widow goddess, is invoked to annihilate internal adversaries: Kama, Krodha, Lobha, Moha, Mada, Matsarya. A pure form of upasana calls for the elimination of all plans of action, a merger into the sacred silence of Sarva Sankalpa Varjanam. In its impure manifestation, Dhumâvati becomes the potent force within tantra—an embodiment of desire executed without delay, lest it befall uncontrollable fear leading to ultimate demise.

## *Sadhana: Manifesting Existence from Non-Existence*

For those adept in the arcane realms of vidyâs, having tasted the nectar of savikalpa samadhi (the mind is conscious only of the Spirit within; it is not conscious of the exterior world. The body is in a trancelike state, but the consciousness is fully perceptive of its blissful experience within) and occasionally glimpsed nirvikalpa samadhi(when the ego has come into an inexorable friendship with the truth    when the love affair of the ego with the Truth has gained stability, a certain permanence), Dhumavati beckons. Her upasana, a sacred journey for the intrepid seeker, unfolds the purpose of sadhana—to manifest the concealed Existence within Non-Existence, to unveil the bliss hidden within the cosmic tapestry of pain. In this intricate dance, the devotee becomes a participant in the cosmic play of creation, dissolution, and the eternal renewal of existence.

# Bagalamukhi:
# The Golden Silence of Stilled Forces

In the vibrant tapestry of divine manifestations, Bagalamukhi stands adorned in resplendent yellow, a hue that transcends mere aesthetics to embody profound symbolism. Clad in the golden radiance of wisdom suppressed, she wields the potent forces of paralyzation, stupefaction, and a striking power that resonates with the profound silence of yellow-imbued contemplation.

### *The Artistry of Silence: Paralyzing the Opponent's Speech*

With a regal demeanor, Bagalamukhi extends her left hand, deftly catching hold of the opponent's tongue, a symbolic gesture that transcends physicality to embody the paralyzing force of speech—vâk stambhankari. In her right hand, a mace poised for action, she becomes the cosmic force stifling the vocal expressions of resistance and dissent.

### *The Radiance of Yellow: A Tapestry of Thoughtful Stillness*

Yellow, the chosen palette of Bagalamukhi's cosmic expression, extends beyond mere adornments. It encapsulates the essence of the thinking mind, a hue that tempers the downpour of intuition and inspiration. In the worship of this resplendent goddess, the worshipper mirrors her golden complexion, adorned in yellow garments, beads of turmeric, and immersed in contemplation that transcends the limits of the mundane.

### *Sri Vidya Connection: Dandanâtha, the Commander of Forces*

Bagalâmukhi, in her cosmic significance, finds resonance in the intricate web of Sri Vidya. She is the counterpart to Dandanâtha, the Commander of the Armed Forces of

Rajarâjeshwari. As the striking force of the Divine Mother, she orchestrates a symphony of immobilization—arresting all movement and activity. Her divine influence induces sudden stillness, a pause in the ceaseless flow of manifestation.

### *The Edifice of Hatha and Raja Yoga: Stopping the Current*

Delving into the intricacies of yogic philosophy, Bagalamukhi's cosmic dance aligns with the principles of Hatha Yoga and Raja Yoga. Like a sudden stemming of a rushing current, she demonstrates the art of arresting the flow of breath—a yogic practice that grants control over pranic energy. In this cosmic pause, the adept yogi gains mastery over the very essence of life, momentarily suspending the laws of nature.

### *The Silence Between Thoughts: The Essence of Raja Yoga*

In the profound corridors of Raja Yoga, Bagalamukhi's influence extends to mental pranayama—the regulation of thoughts akin to the ebb and flow of breath. The space between thoughts becomes the sacred ground for the seeker, a realm where control over the mind is forged by navigating the silent spaces within consciousness.

### *Bagalamukhi's Invocation: A Shift in Destiny's Current*

Worship of Bagalamukhi becomes a transformative journey, a divine dialogue that alters the course of progress toward destiny. In her golden silence, she does not rewrite destiny but, with a cosmic brushstroke, guides the currents towards a destination that aligns with the sacred dance of universal forces. The devotee, draped in the radiance of yellow, becomes a participant in this celestial orchestration—a silent, contemplative partner in the cosmic dance of creation and stillness.

# Matangi:
# Symphony of Manifested Sound

In the celestial hierarchy of the ten Great Vidyas, Matangi emerges as the enchanting embodiment of manifested sound, akin to the illustrious Tara. Her essence transcends the unmanifest sound of Tara, dwelling in the realm of intelligible, vibrant sound—the primordial throb, *Adya Spanda*, that resonates from the self-volition of the Supreme.

### *The Eternal Word: A Cosmic Symphony in Four Movements*

From the ethereal Adya Spanda, a cosmic symphony unfurls, manifesting as Nada—the Eternal Word, the divine Creatrix of manifestation. This symphony takes shape in four steps: sthula (gross, matter principle), sukshma (subtle, life principle), Karana (causal, mind principle), and maha karana (great causal, original rhythm). These steps echo the cosmic dance of waking, dreaming, deep sleep, and transcendental states.

### *Nada in the Nervous System: A Tantric Allegory*

The intricacies of sound find their reflection in the human nervous system according to Tantric wisdom. Para, the supreme source, lies dormant in the muladhara, while pashyanti, the perceiving word, resides in the manipura chakra. Madhyama, the subtle word, weaves its essence between the navel and the throat at the anâhata chakra. Finally, vaikhari, the expressive speech, finds its culmination as the goddess Matangi.

### *Matangi's Radiance: A Green Symphony of Thought*

Matangi, resplendent in her greenish-dark complexion (Syamala), transcends the limitations of mere symbolism. Her tender limbs glow with the radiance of sapphire, embodying the confluence of pristine purity and expressive manifestation. Ucchista Chândâli, signifies the transition of the unmanifest Word, coloured during expression, as it descends from the Supreme Source.

### *Mantrini of Lalita: Attraction and Devotion Unveiled*

In the grand tapestry of divine alliances, Matangi holds the coveted position of *mantrini* to Lalita. Her divine purpose unfolds as the harbinger of attraction, beckoning devotees toward Lalita's cosmic embrace. Matangi, the wielder of akarshana and vashya pradhana shakti, becomes the magnetic force that unites seekers with the divine. Her mantra, a sacred formula, carries a gap—an invitation for devotees to fill it with the name of their desired deity, siddha, or God.

### *Attraction as Devotion: The Celestial Dance of Castes and Colors*

Matangi, the candala kanya, transcends societal norms and barriers. Dark in colour, with a luscious form, she becomes the embodiment of candali—a symbol not only for the unbridled kundalini but also Sushumna in Tantra's Sandhya bhasha. Her worship leads seekers to break through the shackles of caste, creed, and colour, embracing the universal essence that unites all.

### *Matangi's Covenant: Union with the Divine*

Matangi, synonymous with Sarasvati, bestows upon her devotees the fulfillment of desires and the wisdom to discern the transient nature of sensory games. For women, she demands union with a minimum of eight Bhairavas, while men are beckoned to unite with 108, the sacred number echoing the names in Khadgamala. Matangi's intricate path leads seekers to the mandala of Srichakra, where identity and lover become portals to the profound union with Lalita.

### *The Culmination: Identity in the Symphony of Relations*

Matangi, in her grand finale, dismantles the illusion of duality, revealing the truth of identity. In this cosmic revelation, all relations coexist, and God becomes the essence of every conceivable connection—father, mother, brother, sister, lover, and more. The seeker, enveloped in the divine embrace of Matangi, becomes a participant in the celestial symphony where the notes of Jnana and bhakti yoga intertwine, mesmerizing the soul with the eternal sound of existence.

# Kamalatmika:
# Symphony of Divine Abundance

In the celestial tapestry of divinity, Kamalatmika emerges as the quintessence of beauty, abundance, and the ultimate source of joy, strength, and power. She weaves the intricate threads of existence, transforming mortals into reflections of Vishnu, invoking the splendour of creation itself.

### *The Lotus-Born Radiance: Source of All Creation*

Kamalatmika, the resplendent goddess, derives her name from wearing waters as her divine robes, symbolizing the essence of creative consciousness. Cloaked in the waters of infinite potential, she orchestrates the dance of existence. She is the Lady of the Lotus, gracing every step upon the delicate petals, imparting beauty to the very essence of creation.

### *Divine Motherhood: Nourishing the Cosmos*

With two hands delicately cradling lotus flowers and the others bestowing boons while warding off fears, Kamalatmika emanates a luminous golden complexion draped in white silk. Four majestic elephants, as wise as the snowy mountains, shower her with the ambrosial water of immortality, symbolizing sagacity, wisdom, and the creative principle of the cosmos.

### *Sowbhagya Lakshmi: The Embodiment of Blissful Wisdom*

Kamalatmika, also known as Sowbhagya Lakshmi, encapsulates the knowledge of blissful wisdom. Her divine invocation, the Sowbhagye Lakshmi Upanishad, unfolds the path to moksha and aiswarya vidya, revealing the nature of true happiness. She personifies the joyous Ananda of Narayana, embracing all dimensions of space.

### *The Divine Symphony: Samadhi and Union with the Absolute*

Guiding Seekers on the Path to Samadhi, Kamalatmika imparts the wisdom of the nine cakras. From the primal source at the muladhara, through the realms of svadhisthana, manipura, anahata, vishuddha, talu, bhru, Ajna, and culminating at the akasa cakra, she reveals the cosmic dance of union and self-realization.

### *Nirvane Cakra: Liberation and Immortality*

At the Brahma randhram, the cosmic yoni where the creative power of time, Kala, flows to manifest the world, seekers attain liberation and mukti. The ninth cakra, Akasa cakra, unveils the purna giri peetham, fulfilling even the subtlest desires that manifest in the heart of the seeker.

### *Sowbhagya Lakshmi Upanishad: A Purifying Flame*

The daily recitation of the Sowbhagya Lakshmi Upanishad purifies the seeker, aligning them with the elements of fire and air. This sacred knowledge dismantles the illusions of limitations imposed by the external world, unlocking the realization that bliss and freedom reside within.

### *A Universal Blessing: The Invocation of Love and Peace*

May the essence of Kamalatmika's teachings resonate in every heart. May humanity recognize the divinity within, fostering detachment from both pleasure and pain. In this recognition, may the symphony of love, peace, and prosperity prevail, transcending barriers of caste, creed, and belief.

### *The Radiant Vision: All Be One and One Be All*

Let the radiant vision of Kamalatmika be the guiding light, inspiring all to see the same divine consciousness in themselves and others. In this unified vision, may joy reign supreme, tensions subside, and a profound understanding of oneness prevail.

### *A Benediction of Universal Harmony*

May the world witness the diminishing of anger, violence, and strife, giving rise to a shared embrace of joy and liberation. May the spirit of giving, sharing, and unconditional love thrive, nurturing a global tapestry where every individual recognizes their divine essence and the interconnectedness of all existence.

*In the Symphony of Kamalatmika, May All Be One, and One Be All.*

Chapter : 12

# The Yoginis :

There are 64 in total, each with their own unique qualities and powers. These goddesses can be seen as aspects of the ultimate Divine Mother or Shakti, who is believed to be the source of all creation and energy. By connecting with the energies of Yoginis through meditation, rituals, and devotion, one can tap into their own inner strength and wisdom.

The stories and symbolism of Yoginis also serve as powerful reminders of the importance of embracing all aspects of ourselves, regardless of social norms or expectations. Through honouring these powerful feminine energies, we can gain a better understanding of our own divinity and connection to the universal consciousness. So let us bow down to the Yoginis and allow their wisdom to guide us on our spiritual journeys. As we delve deeper into the world of Yoginis, may we also remember to honour and respect the diversity and complexity of femininity in all its forms. Let us embrace our own unique qualities and powers, just like the 64 Yoginis, and allow them to guide us on our journey towards enlightenment and self-discovery. So let us bow down to the Yoginis and allow their wisdom to guide us on our spiritual journeys. May we embody their strength, grace, and divinity in all aspects of our lives, and may we continue to honour and celebrate the divine feminine within ourselves and in the world around us.

Just as each Yogini represents a unique aspect of femininity, we too are all unique individuals who can come together to form a powerful collective energy. Let us support and uplift one another, celebrating the diversity and strength of our shared femininity. Through connection and support, we can tap into even greater depths of wisdom and strength within ourselves.

The Yogini tradition is deeply rooted in Hinduism and Tantric traditions, and it is important to approach these teachings with cultural sensitivity and understanding. By honouring the origins of the Yoginis, we can deepen our connection to their energies and gain a greater appreciation for their significance in spiritual practices.

The yogini tradition also highlights the importance of balance between masculine and feminine energies within each individual. Both are necessary for spiritual growth and enlightenment and must be honoured and nurtured equally.

In today's society, where women still face discrimination and inequality, the yoginis serve as a source of inspiration for empowerment and breaking societal norms. They remind us that true power comes from within, regardless of societal expectations or limitations.

Each of these Yoginis holds a unique significance and offers different blessings to those who worship them. They embody various energies and qualities that can aid

## *Navigating the Mystical Path: Connecting with Yoginis in the Modern Era*

In the contemporary world, where ancient spiritual traditions encounter the complexities of modern life, the approach to connecting with Kali and He 64 Yoginis may seem elusive. Amid the confusion, what remains paramount is the sincere desire to connect, fuelled by genuine devotion, love, and a passion for the mystical. The path to their presence is one of non-duality, transcending the limitations of structured rituals or rigid methodologies.

True connection with the Yoginis often begins with an inner calling, an earnest yearning that aligns with the purity of intention. In the tapestry of nature's wisdom, a sincere seeker, driven by devotion, may find subtle signs and synchronicities guiding them toward these divine beings. The interconnectedness of all things unfolds as a cosmic dance, where each step in devotion resonates with the next, forming a seamless link from the seeker's heart to the realm of the Yoginis.

Embracing the essence of non-duality, the seeker dissolves the boundaries between the sacred and the mundane, recognizing the divine in every aspect of existence. In this approach, the connection is not bound by rigid structures but flows organically, guided by the currents of love and spiritual passion.

Ultimately, the journey to connect with the 64 Yoginis is a dynamic, ever-unfolding process. As the seeker delves deeper into the realms of devotion and non-duality, nature responds, revealing the interconnected threads that weave through the cosmos. In this sacred dance, the seeker and the divine become intertwined, and the Yoginis, in their infinite grace, unveil the path of connection—a path that is as unique as the sincere heart that treads upon it.

It is a dance of energies, a harmonious exchange between the finite and the infinite. As the seeker navigates the realms of devotion and love, the Yoginis, in their myriad forms, respond to the sincere vibrations echoing from the seeker's heart.

In this interconnected web of existence, signs and symbols become messengers, guiding the seeker toward deeper communion. Nature herself orchestrates a silent symphony, unveiling the path to connection through subtle whispers, dreams, or encounters that bear the imprint of divine presence.

The seeker, fuelled by passion, surrenders the egoistic self at the altar of devotion. Here, the Yoginis, with their distinct attributes and mystical significance, become catalysts for transformation. The seeker's journey becomes a pilgrimage of the soul, traversing the landscapes of the sacred and the profane, transcending dualities to unveil the unity inherent in all things.

As the seeker progresses, the armour and forms of the Yoginis cease to be mere adornments; they become gateways to profound understanding. Each attribute and symbol carries layers of meaning, reflecting the seeker's inner landscape and facilitating a dialogue with the divine.

In this dance of devotion, the seeker discovers that true connection is not a destination but a continuous unfoldment. The Yoginis, timeless and omnipresent, respond to the seeker's sincerity, revealing themselves in the subtlest whispers of the wind, the gentle rustling of leaves, and the symphony of the cosmos—a path that leads not only to their presence but also to the depths of the seeker's own soul, where the sacred dance of connection perpetually unfolds.

## *64 Mysteries: The Enigmatic Origin of Yoginis*

The precise origins of the 64 Yoginis are deeply shrouded in the antiquity of spiritual traditions, making it challenging to pinpoint an exact timeframe. However, these divine beings have roots in ancient yogic and tantric practices, likely spanning over several centuries. Their presence can be traced through the rich tapestry of Hindu and tantric literature, suggesting that they have been revered for a significant span of time, possibly over a millennium. The mystical lore surrounding the Yoginis often connects them to the deep currents of spiritual evolution, making their existence timeless and intertwined with the essence of cosmic wisdom.

## *Sacred Lineage of Yoginis: Unveiling Divine Forms and Attributes*

In the mystical tapestry of spiritual exploration, discover the profound significance, attributes, and forms of the revered Yoginis—guides on the path to divine connection. Each Yogini carries a unique essence, inviting seekers into the dance of sacred energies and unveiling the secrets of transformation. Join the pilgrimage to explore the timeless wisdom embedded in the armour, forms, and attributes of these revered beings.

## 1. Kali Nitya Siddhamata:

Attributes: Adorned with a garland of skulls and holding a trident, symbolizing the transformative power of time.

Armor: Clad in celestial armour representing the eternal dance of creation and destruction, adorned with symbols of cosmic forces.

Form: Radiates an aura of fierce grace, with a countenance reflecting both the destructive and nurturing aspects of the divine feminine.

Symbology: Represents eternal motherhood, guiding seekers on the path of Siddhas (perfected beings) towards liberation.

Mystical Significance: Channels the timeless essence of divine wisdom, providing solace and enlightenment to those who surrender to her.

## 2. Kapalini Nagalakshmi:

Attributes: Holds a skull and a lotus, symbolizing the cyclical nature of life and death, and the purity rising from impurity.

Armor: Draped in serpentine attire, representing the kundalini energy, and adorned with serpents as symbols of transformation.

Form: Radiates an aura of both ferocity and grace, with a countenance reflecting the dual nature of life's cycles.

Symbology: Symbolizes the divine serpent energy (Naga), representing the transformative power of spiritual awakening.

Mystical Significance: Leads devotees through the cycles of life, death, and rebirth, guiding towards spiritual enlightenment.

## 3. Kula Devi Svarnadeha:

Attributes: Holds symbols of fertility and abundance, embodying the generative power of the divine feminine.

Armor: Clad in golden attire, symbolizing wealth, prosperity, and the regal aspect of the goddess.

Form: Radiates an aura of maternal abundance, with a countenance reflecting the nurturing and caring aspect of the divine mother.

Symbology: Represents the creative and abundant force of the cosmic mother, providing sustenance to all beings.

Mystical Significance: Bestows devotees with material and spiritual wealth, nurturing them on their journey of life.

## 4. Kurukulla Rasanatha:

Attributes: Holds a bow and arrow, symbolizing the control and direction of desires towards higher spiritual goals.

Armor: Adorned in garments reflecting the colours of passion and desire, embellished with symbols of love and attraction.

Form: Radiates an aura of enchanting beauty, with a countenance reflecting the captivating allure of divine love.

Symbology: Symbolizes the goddess of desire, guiding devotees to harness and redirect their desires towards spiritual evolution.

Mystical Significance: Assists seekers in cultivating divine love, transcending worldly desires and connecting with higher realms.

### 5. Virodhini Vilasini:

Attributes: Holds a mirror, symbolizing self-reflection and inner contemplation.

Armor: Adorned in garments representing the reflective nature of the mind, embellished with symbols of introspection.

Form: Radiates an aura of inner beauty, with a countenance reflecting the serenity achieved through self-awareness.

Symbology: Represents the goddess residing within, guiding devotees to explore the inner realms of consciousness.

Mystical Significance: Facilitates self-discovery, helping seekers find harmony and balance through introspection and inner wisdom.

### 6. Vipracitta Rakta Priya:

Attributes: Holds symbols of passion and love, signifying the joyful embrace of divine sensuality.

Armor: Adorned in garments reflecting the vibrant hues of love, embellished with symbols of romantic allure.

Form: Radiates an aura of passionate energy, with a countenance reflecting the intoxicating essence of divine love.

Symbology: Symbolizes the goddess of romantic love, guiding devotees to experience divine bliss through passionate devotion.

Mystical Significance: Inspires seekers to transcend mundane love, leading them towards a higher, spiritual union with the divine.

## 7. Ugra Rakta Bhoga Rupa:

Attributes: Holds ritual implements symbolizing enjoyment and indulgence in the pleasures of existence.

Armor: Clad in attire representing indulgence in worldly pleasures, adorned with symbols of sensual delight.

Form: Radiates an aura of indulgent bliss, with a countenance reflecting the satisfaction derived from divine pleasures.

Symbology: Represents the goddess of indulgence, guiding devotees to experience divine joy through sensory delights.

Mystical Significance: Teaches seekers to find the sacred in the ordinary, leading them to a deeper connection with divine pleasures.

## 8. Ugraprabha Shukranatha:

Attributes: Holds a vina (musical instrument), symbolizing the harmonious balance of passion and artistic expression.

Armor: Adorned in garments representing the vibrancy of artistic creativity, embellished with symbols of artistic prowess.

Form: Radiates an aura of creative energy, with a countenance reflecting the divine inspiration of artistic endeavours.

Symbology: Symbolizes the goddess of artistic expression, guiding devotees to channel passion into creative pursuits.

Mystical Significance: Inspires seekers to explore their creative potential, fostering a connection with the divine through artistic endeavours.

## 9. Dipa Mukti Rakta Deha:

Attributes: Holds a lamp symbolizing the inner light of knowledge and the liberation attained through wisdom.

Armor: Clad in garments representing the brilliance of inner wisdom, adorned with symbols of enlightenment.

Form: Radiates an aura of illuminated knowledge, with a countenance reflecting the serenity of enlightened consciousness.

Symbology: Represents the goddess of wisdom and enlightenment, guiding devotees towards liberation through knowledge.

Mystical Significance: Illuminates the path of seekers, leading them from darkness to the radiant light of spiritual understanding.

## 10. Neela Bhukti Rakta Sparsha:

Attributes: Holds symbols of sensory perception, signifying the divine experience derived from the touch of passion.

Armor: Adorned in garments reflecting the sensual nature of touch, embellished with symbols of tactile sensation.

Form: Radiates an aura of sensory delight, with a countenance reflecting the ecstasy of divine touch.

Symbology: Symbolizes the goddess of tactile sensation, guiding devotees to experience divine bliss through sensory contact.

Mystical Significance: Teaches seekers to find the sacred in the sensory, leading them to a deeper connection with divine touch.

## 11. Ghana Maha Jagadamba:

Attributes: Holds the universe, symbolizing the cosmic power and motherhood overseeing all aspects of creation.

Armor: Adorned in garments representing the vastness of the cosmos, embellished with cosmic symbols.

Form: Radiates an aura of universal energy, with a countenance reflecting the nurturing essence of cosmic motherhood.

Symbology: Symbolizes the Great Mother of the world, embodying the cosmic energy that sustains and nurtures all life.

Mystical Significance: Invokes the universal nurturing force, guiding seekers towards a harmonious connection with the cosmic order.

## 12. Balaka Kama Sevita:

Attributes: Attended by Kamadeva, the God of Love, symbolizing the divine presence in the realm of romantic love.

Armor: Clad in garments representing the beauty and allure of romantic love, embellished with symbols of romantic attraction.

Form: Radiates an aura of romantic energy, with a countenance reflecting the divine embrace of love.

Symbology: Represents the goddess attended by the God of Love, guiding devotees to experience divine love in all its forms.

Mystical Significance: Inspires seekers to explore the divine aspect of love, leading them towards a deeper connection with the essence of romantic passion.

## 13. Matra Devi Atma Vidya:

Attributes: Holds sacred scriptures, symbolizing the knowledge of the Self and the divine wisdom present in spiritual teachings.

Armor: Adorned in garments representing the purity of spiritual knowledge, embellished with symbols of sacred wisdom.

Form: Radiates an aura of profound wisdom, with a countenance reflecting the divine knowledge of the Self.

Symbology: Symbolizes the goddess with knowledge of the Self, guiding devotees towards self-realization and spiritual wisdom.

Mystical Significance: Illuminates the path of seekers, leading them to a profound understanding of their true nature and the divine within.

## 14. Mudra Purna Raja Kripa:

Attributes: Holds a mudra (hand gesture) symbolizing compassion and divine grace, reflecting the benevolence of the goddess.

Armor: Clad in garments representing the compassion and grace of divine benevolence, embellished with symbols of mercy.

Form: Radiates an aura of divine compassion, with a countenance reflecting the boundless grace of the goddess.

Symbology: Represents the goddess radiating compassion, guiding devotees towards the transformative power of divine grace.

Mystical Significance: Invokes the divine grace that bestows blessings and benevolence, leading seekers towards spiritual transformation.

## 15. Mita Tantra Kaula Diksha:

Attributes: Initiates the Kaula Tantra Path, holding symbols of tantric initiation and the sacred knowledge of the Kaula tradition.

Armor: Adorned in garments representing the sacredness of tantric wisdom, embellished with symbols of esoteric knowledge.

Form: Radiates an aura of tantric energy, with a countenance reflecting the mystical essence of the Kaula tradition.

Symbology: Symbolizes the initiator of the Kaula Tantra Path, guiding devotees towards the esoteric wisdom of tantric practices.

Mystical Significance: Leads seekers into the profound realms of tantric knowledge and initiation, fostering a connection with divine mysteries.

## 16. Maha Kali Siddheshvari:

Attributes: Holds symbols of Siddhi (attainment) and Ishvara (Supreme Being), embodying the ultimate realization of divine power.

Armor: Clad in garments representing the transcendence of material illusions, embellished with symbols of supreme spiritual attainment.

Form: Radiates an aura of absolute power, with a countenance reflecting the supreme realization of divine identity.

Symbology: Symbolizes the Queen of the Siddhas, embodying the highest spiritual attainment and divine realization.

Mystical Significance: Invokes the transformative power of spiritual realization, guiding seekers towards the ultimate attainment of divine identity.

## 17. Kameshwari Sarvashakti:

Attributes: Holds symbols of desire (Kama) and all-encompassing power (Shakti), embodying the divine energy that fulfills all desires.

Armor: Adorned in garments representing the manifestation of desires, embellished with symbols of omnipotent divine power.

Form: Radiates an aura of desire-fulfilling energy, with a countenance reflecting the all-encompassing power of divine Shakti.

Symbology: Represents the Shakti of all, embodying the divine force that fulfills the desires of devotees.

Mystical Significance: Guides seekers to connect with the omnipotent divine power that fulfills their spiritual and material desires.

## 18. Bhagamalini Tarini:

Attributes: Holds symbols of protection and deliverance, embodying the divine force that rescues devotees from calamities.

Armor: Clad in garments representing protective energy, embellished with symbols of safeguarding devotees from harm.

Form: Radiates an aura of protective energy, with a countenance reflecting the compassionate deliverance of the goddess.

Symbology: Symbolizes the goddess who delivers from calamity, protecting and guiding devotees through challenging situations.

Mystical Significance: Invokes the protective and deliverance power of the goddess, ensuring the well-being of devotees in times of need.

## 19. Nitya Klinna Tantraprita:

Attributes: Holds symbols of tantra and displays a loving disposition, embodying the goddess fond of tantric practices and devotion.

Armor: Adorned in garments representing the sacredness of tantra, embellished with symbols of devotion and tantric knowledge.

Form: Radiates an aura of loving devotion and tantric energy, with a countenance reflecting the goddess's fondness for tantric practices.

Symbology: Represents the goddess who is fond of tantra, guiding devotees towards a path of devotion and sacred tantric practices.

Mystical Significance: Invokes the transformative power of tantra and devotion, leading seekers to a deeper connection with divine mysteries.

## 20. Bherunda Tattva Uttama:

Attributes: Holds symbols of sexual fluidity and primordial energy, embodying the divine power related to the essence of creation.

Armor: Clad in garments representing the fluidity of creation, embellished with symbols of primordial energy.

Form: Radiates an aura of creative energy, with a countenance reflecting the primal force of creation.

Symbology: Symbolizes the power of sexual fluidity and the primordial energy of creation, embodying the essence of creative forces.

Mystical Significance: Guides seekers towards understanding and harnessing the creative forces of the universe, fostering a connection with divine creation.

## 21. Vahnivasini Shashini:

Attributes: Holds symbols of fire (Agni) and moon (Shashini), embodying the radiant energy of both fire and the soothing light of the moon.

Armor: Adorned in garments representing the fiery and cooling aspects of energy, embellished with symbols of celestial illumination.

Form: Radiates an aura balancing the intense energy of fire and the calming influence of the moon, with a countenance reflecting celestial grace.

Symbology: Represents the harmonious interplay of fiery and lunar energies, embodying the balance between intensity and serenity.

Mystical Significance: Invokes the balanced energies of fire and moon, guiding seekers to harness the dynamic equilibrium within themselves.

## 22. Mahavajreshvari Rakta Devi:

Attributes: Holds symbols of sensuality and divine passion, embodying the goddess of sensual pleasures and intense desires.

Armor: Clad in garments representing the allure of sensual pleasures, embellished with symbols of passionate divine energy.

Form: Radiates an aura of sensuality and passion, with a countenance reflecting the intensity of divine desires.

Symbology: Symbolizes the goddess of sensuality and passionate desires, embodying the divine force of intense pleasures.

Mystical Significance: Guides seekers to navigate and understand the transformative power of sensual experiences on the path to spiritual realization.

## 23. Shivaduti Adi Shakti:

Attributes: Holds symbols representing feminine energy and the primordial power of creation, embodying the original feminine force.

Armor: Adorned in garments representing the primal feminine energy, embellished with symbols of the creative power of the goddess.

Form: Radiates an aura of primordial feminine energy, with a countenance reflecting the original force of creation.

Symbology: Represents the original feminine energy and creative power, embodying the primal force that sustains the universe.

Mystical Significance: Invokes the primordial energy of the goddess, guiding seekers towards a deeper understanding of the creative forces within existence.

## 24. Tvarita Urdvaretada:

Attributes: Holds symbols of swift movement and upward ecstasy, embodying the goddess who imparts the joy of upward spiritual ascent.

Armor: Clad in garments representing the swift upward movement, embellished with symbols of ecstatic joy.

Form: Radiates an aura of swift and upward-moving energy, with a countenance reflecting the joyous ascent of spiritual realization.

Symbology: Symbolizes the goddess of swift upward movement and joy, embodying the ecstatic bliss of spiritual ascent.

Mystical Significance: Guides seekers towards the joyous experience of spiritual ascent and the swift movement on the path of divine realization.

## 25. Kulasundari Kamini:

Attributes: Holds symbols of desire and beauty, embodying the goddess who personifies desire itself in its most refined form.

Armor: Adorned in garments representing the essence of desire and beauty, embellished with symbols of refined aesthetic allure.

Form: Radiates an aura of refined desire and beauty, with a countenance reflecting the epitome of aesthetic and passionate allure.

Symbology: Represents the goddess who desires itself, embodying the refined essence of aesthetic and passionate allure.

Mystical Significance: Guides seekers towards the understanding and transcendence of desire, leading to a refined connection with divine beauty.

## 26. Nitya Jnana Swarupini:

Attributes: Holds symbols representing eternal knowledge and the embodiment of wisdom, portraying the eternal form of divine knowledge.

Armor: Clad in garments representing the essence of eternal knowledge, embellished with symbols of profound wisdom.

Form: Radiates an aura of eternal knowledge and wisdom, with a countenance reflecting the eternal form of divine understanding.

Symbology: Symbolizes the goddess of eternal knowledge, embodying the timeless essence of profound wisdom.

Mystical Significance: Guides seekers towards the eternal source of knowledge, facilitating a deep connection with divine wisdom.

## 27. Nilapataka Siddhida:

Attributes: Holds symbols of perfection and accomplishment, embodying the goddess who bestows perfection and Siddhis (supernatural powers).

Armor: Adorned in garments representing the embodiment of perfection, embellished with symbols of accomplishment and divine powers.

Form: Radiates an aura of perfection and accomplishment, with a countenance reflecting the embodiment of divine powers.

Symbology: Represents the goddess of perfection and Siddhis, embodying the divine force that bestows supernatural accomplishments.

Mystical Significance: Guides seekers towards the attainment of perfection and spiritual accomplishments through divine grace.

## 28. Vijaya Devi Vasuda:

Attributes: Holds symbols of victory and wealth, embodying the victorious goddess who bestows abundance and prosperity.

Armor: Clad in garments representing the essence of victory and wealth, embellished with symbols of abundant prosperity.

Form: Radiates an aura of victory and prosperity, with a countenance reflecting the victorious aspect of divine abundance.

Symbology: Symbolizes the goddess of victory and wealth, embodying the divine force that brings forth abundant prosperity.

Mystical Significance: Guides seekers towards achieving victory and abundance in all aspects of life through divine blessings.

## 29. Sarvamangala Tantradha:

Attributes: Holds symbols of tantra and bestower of blessings, embodying the goddess who bestows auspiciousness through tantra.

Armor: Adorned in garments representing the essence of tantra and blessings, embellished with symbols of divine auspiciousness.

Form: Radiates an aura of tantra and auspicious blessings, with a countenance reflecting the bestower of divine grace through tantra.

Symbology: Represents the goddess of tantra and blessings, embodying the divine force that brings auspiciousness through sacred practices.

Mystical Significance: Guides seekers towards the attainment of divine auspiciousness through dedicated tantra practices.

## 30. Jwalamalini Nagini:

Attributes: Holds symbols of fire and serpent energy, embodying the goddess who is the radiant fire and serpent goddess.

Armor: Clad in garments representing the essence of fiery and serpent energy, embellished with symbols of divine radiance and serpent power.

Form: Radiates an aura of fiery and serpent energy, with a countenance reflecting the powerful and transformative nature of fire and serpents.

Symbology: Symbolizes the goddess of fiery and serpent energy, embodying the divine force that transforms through radiant fire and serpent power.

Mystical Significance: Guides seekers towards the transformative power of divine fire and serpent energy in spiritual evolution.

## 31. Citra Devi Rakta Puja:

Attributes: Holds symbols of vibrant colours and passionate worship, embodying the goddess worshipped with fervent devotion and vibrant rituals.

Armor: Adorned in garments representing vibrant hues and symbols of passionate worship, reflecting the essence of intense devotion.

Form: Radiates an aura of vibrant colours and divine passion, with a countenance reflecting the goddess worshipped with fervour.

Symbology: Symbolizes the goddess of intense worship, embodying the divine force that responds to passionate devotion and rituals.

Mystical Significance: Guides seekers towards deepening their spiritual connection through passionate and vibrant worship.

## 32. Lalita Kanya Sukrada:

Attributes: Holds symbols of purity and divine maidenhood, embodying the pure and benevolent goddess who bestows blessings.

Armor: Clad in garments representing the essence of purity and divine maidenhood, embellished with symbols of divine benevolence.

Form: Radiates an aura of purity and divine grace, with a countenance reflecting the benevolent aspect of divine maidenhood.

Symbology: Represents the goddess of purity and blessings, embodying the divine force that blesses with purity and benevolence.

Mystical Significance: Guides seekers towards purity and divine grace through the blessings of the pure and benevolent goddess.

## 33. Dakini Madashalini:

Attributes: Holds symbols of intoxication and blissful rapture, embodying the goddess shining with ecstatic bliss.

Armor: Adorned in garments representing the essence of intoxication and blissful rapture, embellished with symbols of divine ecstasy.

Form: Radiates an aura of intoxication and bliss, with a countenance reflecting the goddess shining with divine ecstasy.

Symbology: Symbolizes the goddess of ecstatic bliss, embodying the divine force that leads to spiritual intoxication and blissful rapture.

Mystical Significance: Guides seekers towards the ecstatic realms of spiritual bliss through divine intoxication.

## 34. Rakini Papa Rasiini:

Attributes: Holds symbols of destruction and dispelling sins, embodying the goddess who is the destroyer of sins.

Armor: Clad in garments representing the essence of destruction and dispelling sins, embellished with symbols of sin-purging power.

Form: Radiates an aura of destructive power and sin-dispelling energy, with a countenance reflecting the goddess who annihilates sins.

Symbology: Represents the goddess of destruction and sin-dispelling, embodying the divine force that eradicates sins and impurities.

Mystical Significance: Guides seekers towards liberation from sins and impurities through the purifying power of the sin-dispelling goddess.

## 35. Lakini Sarva Tantresi:

Attributes: Holds symbols of tantra and rulership, embodying the goddess who is the ruler of all tantras.

Armor: Adorned in garments representing the essence of tantra and rulership, embellished with symbols of supreme authority over all tantras.

Form: Radiates an aura of tantra and divine rulership, with a countenance reflecting the goddess as the supreme authority over all tantric practices.

Symbology: Symbolizes the goddess of tantra and rulership, embodying the divine force that governs and guides all tantric paths.

Mystical Significance: Guides seekers towards mastery and divine guidance on all tantric practices.

### 36. Kakini Naga Nartaki:

Attributes: Holds symbols of dance and serpentine grace, embodying the goddess who dances with Nāgarāja, the serpent deity.

Armor: Clad in garments representing the essence of dance and serpentine grace, embellished with symbols of divine dance and serpent energy.

Form: Radiates an aura of dance and serpentine beauty, with a countenance reflecting the goddess in a divine dance with Nāgarāja.

Symbology: Symbolizes the goddess of dance and serpent energy, embodying the divine force that harmonizes with the serpent deity in celestial dance.

Mystical Significance: Guides seekers towards the rhythm of cosmic dance and serpentine energy through the divine dance with Nāgarāja.

## 37. Sakini Mitra Rupini:

Attributes: Holds symbols of friendship and universal form, embodying the goddess who is a friend to all.

Armor: Adorned in garments representing the essence of friendship and universal form, embellished with symbols of universal friendship.

Form: Radiates an aura of friendliness and universal grace, with a countenance reflecting the goddess as a friend to all beings.

Symbology: Represents the goddess of friendship and universal form, embodying the divine force that extends friendship to all creation.

Mystical Significance: Guides seekers towards universal friendship and divine grace through the goddess who is a friend to all.

## 38. Hakini Manoharini:

Attributes: Holds symbols of mind control and enchanting beauty, embodying the goddess who captivates and steals minds.

Armor: Clad in garments representing the essence of mind control and enchanting beauty, embellished with symbols of irresistible charm.

Form: Radiates an aura of mind-controlling beauty, with a countenance reflecting the goddess who captivates and steals the minds of devotees.

Symbology: Symbolizes the goddess of mind control and enchanting allure, embodying the divine force that captures the minds of seekers.

Mystical Significance: Guides seekers towards the art of mind control and enchantment through the captivating beauty of the mind-stealing goddess.

## 39. Tara Yoga Rakta Purna:

Attributes: Holds symbols of union and complete passion, embodying the goddess who, in union, bestows complete passion.

Armor: Adorned in garments representing the essence of union and complete passion, embellished with symbols of divine passion.

Form: Radiates an aura of union and passionate completeness, with a countenance reflecting the goddess bestowing complete passion in divine union.

Symbology: Represents the goddess of union and complete passion, embodying the divine force that grants total passion in the state of union.

Mystical Significance: Guides seekers towards the realization of complete passion through divine union with the goddess.

## 40. Shodashi Latika Devi:

Attributes: Holds symbols of floral beauty and creeper grace, embodying the goddess who is the creeper goddess.

Armor: Clad in garments representing the essence of floral beauty and creeper grace, adorned with symbols of divine blossoming.

Form: Radiates an aura of floral beauty and creeper elegance, with a countenance reflecting the goddess as the embodiment of divine blossoming.

Symbology: Symbolizes the goddess of floral beauty and creeper grace, embodying the divine force that signifies the blossoming of spiritual consciousness.

Mystical Significance: Guides seekers towards the path of spiritual blossoming through the divine grace of the creeper goddess.

## 41. Bhuvaneshwari Mantrini:

Attributes: Holds symbols of mantra and cosmic energy, embodying the goddess who is the energy of mantra.

Armor: Adorned in garments representing the essence of mantra and cosmic energy, embellished with symbols of divine sound.

Form: Radiates an aura of mantra and cosmic resonance, with a countenance reflecting the goddess as the embodiment of divine sound.

Symbology: Represents the goddess of mantra and cosmic energy, embodying the divine force that resonates through the cosmic vibrations of mantra.

Mystical Significance: Guides seekers towards the transformative power of mantra and cosmic energy through the energy of the mantra goddess.

## 42. Chinnamasta Yoni Vega:

Attributes: Holds symbols of yoni and the power of orgasm, embodying the goddess with a dripping yoni.

Armor: Clad in garments representing the essence of yoni and the energy of orgasm, adorned with symbols of divine fertility.

Form: Radiates an aura of yoni and the potency of orgasmic energy, with a countenance reflecting the goddess with a dripping yoni.

Symbology: Symbolizes the goddess of yoni and the power of orgasm, embodying the divine force that signifies the generative power of creation.

Mystical Significance: Guides seekers towards understanding the creative force of yoni and the transformative energy of orgasm.

## 43. Bhairavi Satya Shukrini:

Attributes: Holds symbols of purity and sensuality, embodying the goddess who is supreme purity.

Armor: Adorned in garments representing the essence of purity and sensuality, embellished with symbols of divine purity.

Form: Radiates an aura of purity and sensuous grace, with a countenance reflecting the goddess as the embodiment of supreme purity.

Symbology: Represents the goddess of purity and sensuality, embodying the divine force that signifies the union of spiritual purity and sensuous beauty.

Mystical Significance: Guides seekers towards the path of spiritual purity and sensuous refinement through the embodiment of supreme purity.

## 44. Dhumavati Kundalini:

Attributes: Holds symbols of Kundalini energy, embodying the primordial energy of the Self.

Armor: Clad in garments representing the essence of Kundalini energy, adorned with symbols of divine spiritual awakening.

Form: Radiates an aura of Kundalini energy and spiritual awakening, with a countenance reflecting the goddess as the embodiment of primordial energy.

Symbology: Symbolizes the goddess of Kundalini energy, embodying the divine force that signifies the awakening and ascension of spiritual energy.

Mystical Significance: Guides seekers towards the realization of spiritual potential and the awakening of Kundalini energy for higher consciousness.

## 45. Bagalamukhi Gurumurti:

Attributes: Holds symbols of the guru and divine control, embodying the goddess in the form of the Guru.

Armor: Adorned in garments representing the essence of the guru and divine control, embellished with symbols of divine authority.

Form: Radiates an aura of the guru and divine control, with a countenance reflecting the goddess as the embodiment of divine guidance.

Symbology: Represents the goddess in the form of the Guru, embodying the divine force that signifies control and mastery over adversities.

Mystical Significance: Guides seekers towards divine control and mastery over challenges through the embodiment of the Guru.

## 46. Matangi Kanta Yuvati:

Attributes: Holds symbols of youthful beauty and love, embodying the goddess of youthful beauty enhanced by love.

Armor: Clad in garments representing the essence of youthful beauty and love, adorned with symbols of divine love.

Form: Radiates an aura of youthful beauty and love, with a countenance reflecting the goddess as the embodiment of love and beauty.

Symbology: Symbolizes the goddess of youthful beauty enhanced by love, embodying the divine force that signifies the beauty and vitality of divine love.

Mystical Significance: Guides seekers towards experiencing divine love and beauty through the embodiment of youthful grace.

## 47. Kamala Shukla Samsthita:

Attributes: Holds symbols of lotus and pure existence, embodying the goddess who resides in the semen.

Armor: Adorned in garments representing the essence of lotus and pure existence, embellished with symbols of divine purity.

Form: Radiates an aura of lotus and pure existence, with a countenance reflecting the goddess as the embodiment of divine purity.

Symbology: Represents the goddess who resides in the semen, embodying the divine force that signifies the purity and potential of creation.

Mystical Significance: Guides seekers towards recognizing the divine essence within creation through the embodiment of pure existence.

## 48. Prakriti Brahmandri Devi:

Attributes: Holds symbols of the crown and cosmic consciousness, embodying the goddess who resides in the crown.

Armor: Clad in garments representing the essence of the crown and cosmic consciousness, adorned with symbols of divine cosmic awareness.

Form: Radiates an aura of the crown and cosmic consciousness, with a countenance reflecting the goddess as the embodiment of cosmic awareness.

Symbology: Symbolizes the goddess who resides in the crown, embodying the divine force that signifies the union of individual and cosmic consciousness.

Mystical Significance: Guides seekers towards attaining cosmic consciousness through the embodiment of the goddess in the crown.

## 49. Gayatri Nitya Citrini:

Attributes: Holds symbols of the eternal light within Suṣumṇā, embodying the goddess who is the eternal light of Self.

Armor: Adorned in garments representing the essence of eternal light and Self-awareness, embellished with symbols of divine illumination.

Form: Radiates an aura of eternal light within Suṣumṇā, with a countenance reflecting the goddess as the embodiment of Self-illumination.

Symbology: Symbolizes the goddess who is the eternal light of Self within Suṣumṇā, embodying the divine force that signifies the inner illumination of the Self.

Mystical Significance: Guides seekers towards self-awareness and inner illumination through the embodiment of the eternal light within Suṣumṇā.

## 50. Mohini Matta Yogini:

Attributes: Holds symbols of intoxication, embodying the goddess who is intoxicated.

Armor: Clad in garments representing the essence of intoxication, adorned with symbols of divine ecstasy.

Form: Radiates an aura of intoxication, with a countenance reflecting the goddess as the embodiment of ecstatic bliss.

Symbology: Represents the goddess who is intoxicated, embodying the divine force that signifies the blissful ecstasy of spiritual intoxication.

Mystical Significance: Guides seekers towards experiencing divine ecstasy and bliss through the embodiment of the intoxicated goddess.

## 51. Saraswati Svarga Devi:

Attributes: Holds symbols of the celestial realm, embodying the goddess who is the goddess of heaven.

Armor: Adorned in garments representing the essence of the celestial realm, embellished with symbols of divine grace.

Form: Radiates an aura of the celestial realm, with a countenance reflecting the goddess as the embodiment of heavenly grace.

Symbology: Symbolizes the goddess of heaven, embodying the divine force that signifies the grace and blessings from celestial realms.

Mystical Significance: Guides seekers towards receiving divine blessings and grace through the embodiment of the goddess of heaven.

## 52. Annapurna Shiva Sangi:

Attributes: Holds symbols of nourishment and divine union with Shiva, embodying the goddess who is always with Śiva.

Armor: Clad in garments representing the essence of nourishment and divine union, adorned with symbols of divine sustenance.

Form: Radiates an aura of nourishment and divine union, with a countenance reflecting the goddess as the embodiment of divine sustenance.

Symbology: Represents the goddess who is always with Śiva, embodying the divine force that signifies the union and nourishment derived from divine presence.

Mystical Significance: Guides seekers towards divine sustenance and union through the embodiment of the goddess always with Śiva.

## 53. Narasimhi Vama Devi:

Attributes: Holds symbols of ferocity and protection, embodying the goddess who is the beloved and ferocious protector.

Armor: Adorned in garments representing the essence of ferocity and protection, embellished with symbols of divine fierceness.

Form: Radiates an aura of ferocity and protection, with a countenance reflecting the goddess as the embodiment of divine fierceness.

Symbology: Symbolizes the goddess who is the beloved and ferocious protector, embodying the divine force that signifies the fierce protection of devotees.

Mystical Significance: Guides seekers towards seeking divine protection and fierce love through the embodiment of the beloved and ferocious goddess.

### 54. Ganga Yoni Swarupini:

Attributes: Holds symbols of the yoni and divine energy, embodying the goddess who is the energy of the yoni.

Armor: Clad in garments representing the essence of the yoni and divine energy, adorned with symbols of divine creation.

Form: Radiates an aura of the yoni and divine energy, with a countenance reflecting the goddess as the embodiment of creative energy.

Symbology: Represents the goddess who is the energy of the yoni, embodying the divine force that signifies the creative energy within creation.

Mystical Significance: Guides seekers towards recognizing the divine creative energy through the embodiment of the goddess as the energy of the yoni.

## 55. Aparajita Samaptida:

Attributes: Holds symbols of victory and completion, embodying the goddess who is the energy of victory.

Armor: Adorned in garments representing the essence of victory and completion, embellished with symbols of triumph.

Form: Radiates an aura of victory and completion, with a countenance reflecting the goddess as the embodiment of triumphant energy.

Symbology: Symbolizes the goddess who is the energy of victory, embodying the divine force that signifies the triumph over challenges and completion.

Mystical Significance: Guides seekers towards achieving victory and completeness through the embodiment of the goddess as the energy of triumph.

## 56. Chamunda Parianga Natha:

Attributes: Holds symbols of sacred erection and rulership, embodying the goddess who is the ruler of sacred erection.

Armor: Clad in garments representing the essence of sacred erection and rulership, adorned with symbols of divine rulership.

Form: Radiates an aura of sacred erection and rulership, with a countenance reflecting the goddess as the embodiment of divine rulership.

Symbology: Represents the goddess who is the ruler of sacred erection, embodying the divine force that signifies sacred energy and rulership.

Mystical Significance: Guides seekers towards understanding sacred energy and divine rulership through the embodiment of the goddess as the ruler of sacred erection.

## 57. Varahi Satya Ekakini:

Attributes: Holds symbols of truth and oneness, embodying the goddess who is the oneness of truth.

Armor: Adorned in garments representing the essence of truth and oneness, embellished with symbols of divine truthfulness.

Form: Radiates an aura of truth and oneness, with a countenance reflecting the goddess as the embodiment of divine truth.

Symbology: Symbolizes the goddess who is the oneness of truth, embodying the divine force that signifies the unity of truthfulness.

Mystical Significance: Guides seekers towards embracing truth and oneness through the embodiment of the goddess as the oneness of truth.

## 58. Kaumari Kriya Shaktini:

Attributes: Holds symbols of dedicated action and energy, embodying the goddess who is the energy of dedicated action.

Armor: Clad in garments representing the essence of dedicated action and energy, adorned with symbols of divine vigour.

Form: Radiates an aura of dedicated action and energy, with a countenance reflecting the goddess as the embodiment of dynamic energy.

Symbology: Represents the goddess who is the energy of dedicated action, embodying the divine force that signifies focused and dynamic action.

Mystical Significance: Guides seekers towards engaging in dedicated action and harnessing divine energy through the embodiment of the goddess as the energy of dedicated action.

### 59. Indrani Mukti Niyantri:

Attributes: Holds symbols of guidance and bliss, embodying the goddess who is the guide to bliss.

Armor: Adorned in garments representing the essence of guidance and bliss, embellished with symbols of divine joy.

Form: Radiates an aura of guidance and bliss, with a countenance reflecting the goddess as the embodiment of blissful guidance.

Symbology: Symbolizes the goddess who is the guide to bliss, embodying the divine force that signifies leading seekers towards joyful liberation.

Mystical Significance: Guides seekers towards blissful liberation through the embodiment of the goddess as the guide to bliss.

### 60. Brahmani Ananda Moorti:

Attributes: Holds symbols of bliss and divine form, embodying the goddess who is the image of bliss.

Armor: Clad in garments representing the essence of bliss and divine form, adorned with symbols of divine beauty.

Form: Radiates an aura of bliss and divine form, with a countenance reflecting the goddess as the embodiment of divine beauty and bliss.

Symbology: Represents the goddess who is the image of bliss, embodying the divine force that signifies the beauty and bliss inherent in divine forms.

Mystical Significance: Guides seekers towards experiencing divine beauty and bliss through the embodiment of the goddess as the image of bliss.

## 61. Vaishnavi Satya Rupini:

Attributes: Holds symbols of truth and divine form, embodying the goddess who is the form of truth.

Armor: Adorned in garments representing the essence of truth and divine form, embellished with symbols of divine beauty.

Form: Radiates an aura of truth and divine form, with a countenance reflecting the goddess as the embodiment of divine truth and beauty.

Symbology: Symbolizes the goddess who is the form of truth, embodying the divine force that signifies the truth and beauty inherent in divine forms.

Mystical Significance: Guides seekers towards recognizing divine truth and beauty through the embodiment of the goddess as the form of truth.

## 62. Maheshwari Para Shakti:

Attributes: Holds symbols of transcendental energy, embodying the goddess who is transcendental energy.

Armor: Clad in garments representing the essence of transcendental energy, adorned with symbols of divine transcendence.

Form: Radiates an aura of transcendental energy, with a countenance reflecting the goddess as the embodiment of divine transcendence.

Symbology: Represents the goddess who is transcendental energy, embodying the divine force that signifies the boundless and transcendent nature of divine energy.

Mystical Significance: Guides seekers towards recognizing and connecting with divine transcendental energy through the embodiment of the goddess as transcendental energy.

## 63. Lakshmi Manorama Yoni:

Attributes: Holds symbols of beauty and the divine yoni, embodying the goddess of beautiful yoni.

Armor: Adorned in garments representing the essence of beauty and the divine yoni, embellished with symbols of divine feminine beauty.

Form: Radiates an aura of beauty and the divine yoni, with a countenance reflecting the goddess as the embodiment of divine feminine beauty.

Symbology: Symbolizes the goddess of beautiful yoni, embodying the divine force that signifies the beauty and sacredness of the feminine aspect.

Mystical Significance: Guides seekers towards recognizing the divine beauty and sacredness of the feminine through the embodiment of the goddess as the goddess of beautiful yoni.

### 64. Durga Sachchidananda:

Attributes: Holds symbols of truth, consciousness, and bliss, embodying the goddess who is truth consciousness and bliss.

Armor: Clad in garments representing the essence of truth, consciousness, and bliss, adorned with symbols of divine awareness and joy.

Form: Radiates an aura of truth, consciousness, and bliss, with a countenance reflecting the goddess as the embodiment of divine awareness and joy.

Symbology: Represents the goddess who is truth consciousness and bliss, embodying the divine force that signifies the inseparable union of truth

Mystical Significance: Embodies the trinity of existence, consciousness, and bliss. Her name echoes the eternal truth (Sachchidananda) that transcends the material realm. As the formless reality, she grants seekers a direct experience of divine consciousness, guiding them beyond the illusion of separateness into the boundless ocean of bliss.

## *Role of the 64 Yoginis in Worship and Tantra*

Each Yogini embodies a specific aspect of divine energy, ranging from aspects of nature and creation to qualities like wisdom, strength, love, and transformation.

The 64 Yoginis, in association with a major deity, represent the integration and synthesis of various divine aspects. Their presence symbolizes the multifaceted nature of the divine and the interconnectedness of all aspects of existence.

In Tantric practices, the Yoginis are often invoked for their specific energies and qualities. They are considered powerful aides in spiritual practices, aiding in the practitioner's journey towards enlightenment.

Temples dedicated to the 64 Yoginis, found in various parts of India, are of significant architectural and ritualistic importance. These temples often have a circular design, symbolizing the universe, with each Yogini statue holding a specific position and significance.

The 64 Yoginis are also seen as symbols of female empowerment. Their worship is considered a celebration of the divine feminine, an integral aspect of the balance within the universe.

The association of the 64 Yoginis with major deities underscores the importance of the divine feminine in Hindu and Tantric traditions. It reflects a worldview where the universe is seen as an interplay of diverse yet unified energies, each essential to the cosmic whole. The 64 Yoginis serve as a reminder of this diversity within unity, guiding devotees in their spiritual journeys through their varied and profound energies.

## Veiled Mysteries - Exploring the Kama Kalas in the Realm of Kali and Her Yoginis

In the dance of the cosmos, where each step is a mystery unveiled, we explore the Kama Kalas - the subtle art forms of creation and transformation, under the guiding light of Kali and Her Yoginis.

### Symbolic Significance of the Number 64

In Hindu cosmology, numbers often have symbolic meanings. The number 64 is considered a representation of completeness and wholeness, signifying the full spectrum of cosmic manifestation.

In Tantra, numbers are used to represent certain aspects of the universe and consciousness. The 64 Yoginis symbolize the 64 forms of the divine feminine energy, each embodying unique qualities and aspects of the universe.

Some interpretations relate the 64 Yoginis to the subtle body system, particularly the chakras or energy centers. They are seen as energies that assist in the activation and balancing of these chakras.

The number 64 is also linked to astrological and celestial calculations in Hindu astrology, which plays a significant role in rituals and spiritual practices.

*Chapter : 13*

# The Mystique of Kama Kala: Exploring the Esoteric Realms

### *Unveiling the Essence of Kama Kala*

In the rich tapestry of Hindu and Tantric traditions, the concept of Kama Kala holds a profound place. Distinct from the 64 Yoginis, Kama Kala represents a nuanced and esoteric aspect of Tantra, often associated with the creative and transformative powers of the universe. This chapter delves into the intricate nature of Kama Kala, exploring its significance, symbolism, and role in spiritual practices.

### *The Threefold Nature of Kama Kala*

Kama Kala is primarily understood in a threefold aspect, each representing a fundamental cosmic principle:

Iccha Kala: Symbolizing the divine will or desire, Iccha Kala is the initiating force behind creation. It represents the unmanifested, the seed of potential that precedes all forms and manifestations.

Jnana Kala: This aspect signifies divine knowledge or wisdom. Jnana Kala is the guiding force that directs the creative energy, shaping it into form and structure. It is the principle that brings order to the cosmos.

Kriya Kala: Representing divine action, Kriya Kala is the force of manifestation. It is through Kriya Kala that the divine will is actualized in the physical realm, resulting in the creation and evolution of the universe.

### *Kama Kala and the Divine Feminine*

Kama Kala is deeply connected to the worship of the Divine Feminine, particularly in Shakti and Shakta traditions. It is often seen as an expression of the Goddess's power and creativity. The interplay of these three aspects of Kama Kala symbolizes the dynamic and ever-evolving nature of the universe, constantly shaped by divine will, knowledge, and action.

### *Symbolism in Art and Iconography*

In Hindu iconography, Kama Kala is sometimes depicted as a bindu (dot) or a triangle, each symbol representing its subtle and profound nature. These symbols are key components in various Tantric rituals and meditations, serving as focal points for the practitioner's spiritual journey.

### *Kama Kala in Tantric Practices*

In Tantra, the understanding and meditation of Kama Kala are considered highly esoteric practices, often reserved for advanced practitioners. These practices involve deep meditation, visualization, and mantric chanting, focusing on the union of these cosmic principles and the realization of their presence within the self.

### *The Philosophical Dimensions of Kama Kala*

Philosophically, Kama Kala invites contemplation on the nature of reality, creation, and the interplay of consciousness and energy. It encourages a deeper understanding of the universe not as a static entity but as a dynamic, ever-unfolding expression of divine creativity.

### Conclusion: Embracing the Mysteries of Kama Kala

Kama Kala, with its profound symbolism and deep philosophical implications, offers a gateway to understanding the mysteries of creation and the divine play of consciousness. It challenges practitioners to go beyond the surface and explore the deeper realms of spiritual knowledge. By engaging with the principles of Kama Kala, one embarks on a journey of self-discovery, realizing the interconnectedness of all existence and the dynamic dance of creation that resonates within each individual and the cosmos at large.

### Delving into the Depths of Kama Kala: Iccha, Jnana, and Kriya

### The Triadic Essence of Creation

In the realm of Tantric philosophy, the concept of Kama Kala presents a profound understanding of the cosmos through its three fundamental aspects: Iccha Kala, Jnana Kala, and Kriya Kala. Each of these aspects represents a crucial dimension of the divine process of creation and existence. This chapter explores these three facets in detail, unravelling their intricate interplay in the cosmic dance.

### Iccha Kala: The Seed of Divine Desire

Iccha Kala, often translated as the principle of divine will or desire, stands at the inception of creation. It is the initial spark, the unmanifest potential that precedes all forms and existence.

***The Unmanifested Potential:*** Iccha Kala is akin to a seed that holds within it the blueprint of creation. It is the unseen, unfelt potential that is the source of all that is to manifest.

***The Initiation of the Cosmic Dance:*** This aspect is the divine impulse or intention that begins the cosmic dance. It is the first stir of consciousness that initiates the process of creation.

***Spiritual Significance:*** In spiritual practice, meditation on Iccha Kala involves connecting with the realm of pure potentiality. It is an exercise in understanding and aligning with the divine will, transcending personal desires and ego.

### *Jnana Kala: The Guiding Light of Wisdom*

Jnana Kala represents divine knowledge or wisdom. It is the guiding principle that shapes and directs the energy of creation.

***The Architect of the Universe:*** Jnana Kala provides the blueprint for creation, turning divine will into a discernible form. It is the wisdom that organizes chaos in the cosmos.

***The Illumination of Consciousness:*** This principle is akin to the light of consciousness that illuminates the path of creation, ensuring that the unfolding of the universe is in harmony with the divine plan.

***Path to Enlightenment:*** In the practice of Tantra, focusing on Jnana Kala involves the pursuit of spiritual knowledge and enlightenment. It is about seeking the inner wisdom that aligns one's personal consciousness with the universal consciousness.

## *Kriya Kala: The Manifestation of Divine Action*

Kriya Kala is the principle of divine action, the force that brings the intentions and plans into physical existence.

**The Cosmic Artisan:** Kriya Kala is the dynamic energy that actualizes potential into form. It is the movement from the unmanifest to the manifest, from idea to reality.

**The Dance of Creation:** This aspect symbolizes the active phase of creation, where energy takes shape, and forms evolve. It is the ongoing process of creation and transformation that sustains the universe.

**Engagement with the World:** In Tantric practice, engaging with Kriya Kala involves taking action in the world in alignment with divine will and wisdom. It represents the path of living one's spiritual principles, embodying the divine energy in everyday life.

## *The Triadic Harmony of Existence*

Iccha Kala, Jnana Kala, and Kriya Kala together form a harmonious triad that encapsulates the essence of the divine process of creation. Understanding and meditating upon these aspects offers profound insights into the nature of existence and the role of human consciousness within it. It is a journey that invites practitioners to explore the depths of their being, align with the cosmic rhythm, and participate in the ongoing creation of the universe. This exploration of Iccha, Jnana, and Kriya Kala thus becomes a path to understanding the intricate dance of life and the role of the individual within this vast, dynamic cosmos.

*Chapter : 14*

# The Luminous Paths of Chandra Kala and Surya Kala

### *Illuminating the Twin Energies*

In the realm of Tantra and Yogic philosophy, Chandra Kala and Surya Kala are concepts of profound significance, representing the dual energies that govern various aspects of existence and spiritual practice. These two Kalas, or 'parts,' epitomize the balancing forces in the universe, much like the Yin and Yang in Taoist philosophy. This chapter explores the intricacies of Chandra Kala and Surya Kala, unraveling their meanings, symbolism, and roles in spiritual practices.

### *Chandra Kala: The Lunar Essence*

Chandra Kala, often associated with the moon (Chandra in Sanskrit), symbolizes the cooling, feminine, and receptive aspects of energy. It is an embodiment of the lunar qualities in nature and the human psyche.

**Qualities and Symbolism:** Chandra Kala is reflective, introspective, and associated with the subconscious mind. It represents the nurturing, calming energy that is often linked with creativity, healing, and intuition.

***Spiritual Implications:*** In yogic practices, Chandra Kala is associated with the Ida Nadi, the energy channel that runs along the left side of the spinal column. It is considered the pathway of mental energy and is often linked to lunar, or more passive, meditative states of consciousness.

***Role in Tantra and Yoga:*** Meditations and practices that focus on Chandra Kala are aimed at cultivating inner calm, emotional balance, and heightened intuition. These practices often involve techniques that cool the body and calm the mind, like certain breathing exercises (pranayama) and moon salutations (Chandra Namaskar) in yoga.

The Chandra Kalas, associated with the lunar phases, typically number sixteen, each representing a particular aspect of lunar energy and spiritual significance. Here are their names along with brief symbolic meanings:

1. Amrita - Nectar or divine bliss.
2. Manada - Bestowing honour.
3. Pooshni - Nourishing, providing strength.
4. Tushti - Pleasure or satisfaction.
5. Pushti - Growth, nurturing.
6. Rati - Enjoyment, delight.
7. Dhriti - Courage or steadiness.
8. Shashini - Having the quality of the moon.
9. Chandrika - Moonlight, glowing.
10. Kanta - Radiance or brightness.
11. Jyotsna - Illuminating or moonlit night.
12. Shri - Prosperity, auspiciousness.

13. Priti - Affection, love.
14. Angada - Enhancing, ornamenting.
15. Purna - Fullness, completeness.
16. Poornamrita - Full nectar, the epitome of bliss.

### *Surya Kala: The Solar Vitality*

In contrast, Surya Kala is related to the sun (Surya in Sanskrit) and embodies the dynamic, masculine, and active energy. It represents the solar qualities of illumination, power, and action.

***Qualities and Symbolism:*** Surya Kala is associated with vitality, vigor, and the conscious mind. It symbolizes the active, radiant energy that fuels growth, clarity, and physical strength.

***Spiritual Implications:*** In yogic terms, Surya Kala correlates with the Pingala Nadi, the energy channel running along the right side of the spine. This channel is linked to solar energy and is considered the pathway of physical and vital energy.

***Role in Tantra and Yoga:*** Practices focusing on Surya Kala are designed to stimulate and energize the body and mind. These include specific asanas (postures), vigorous breathing techniques, and sun salutations (Surya Namaskar), all aimed at enhancing physical vitality and mental clarity.

The Surya Kalas, related to solar energy, are also typically enumerated as twelve, but a special 4 added( found in some traditions, and not found in some). Each Kala represents a different aspect of solar energy and its influence. Their names and symbolic meanings are as follows:

## Balancing Chandra and Surya Kalas

The balance between Chandra Kala and Surya Kala is crucial. This equilibrium is essential for holistic well-being, harmonizing the mental (Chandra) and physical (Surya) aspects of our existence. Many yogic and Tantric practices are aimed at achieving this balance, recognizing that spiritual growth requires the integration of both lunar and solar energies.

Understanding and working with Chandra Kala and Surya Kala invites us into a deeper awareness of the dual nature of our existence. These two forces, lunar and solar, are not in opposition but are complementary aspects of the same cosmic energy. By exploring and integrating these energies, we can achieve a state of balance and harmony, not just within ourselves but with the universe at large. The journey through the paths of Chandra Kala and Surya Kala is thus a journey of self-discovery, a dance of light and shadow, stillness and action, intuition and intellect.

The traditional Hindu and Tantric scriptures describe the Chandra Kalas and Surya Kalas as specific aspects or phases of the moon and sun, respectively. Each of these Kalas carries a distinct name and represents various energies or attributes. However, it's important to note that the specific names and interpretations of these Kalas can vary across different texts and traditions.

## Surya Kalas

The Surya Kalas, related to solar energy, are also typically enumerated as sixteen. Each Kala represents a different aspect of solar energy and its influence. Their names and symbolic meanings are as follows:

1. Tapani: The Kala represents the warming, nurturing energy of the sun. It symbolizes the gentle aspect of solar heat.

2. Taapini: This Kala signifies intense solar heat or energy. It is associated with the sun's power to energize and stimulate growth.

3. Dhumraa: Meaning smoky or misty, Dhumraa represents the diffusive aspect of sunlight, perhaps indicating early morning or twilight times when the sun's light is less direct.

4. Marichi: Signifying a ray or beam of light, Marichi embodies the sun's penetrating and illuminating aspect, akin to individual rays of sunlight.

5. Jvalini: This Kala is indicative of the flaming, blazing quality of the sun. Jvalini represents the sun at its most intense and powerful state.

6. Ruchi: Ruchi stands for the lustre and splendor of the sun, its aspect of providing light and clarity.

7. Sushumna: Often associated with the central energy channel in the human body in yogic texts, Sushumna as a solar Kala could represent the balanced, harmonizing energy of the sun.

8. Bhogadaa: Symbolizing enjoyment or pleasure, Bhogadaa may represent the nourishing, life-giving aspects of sunlight that make life enjoyable and fruitful.

9. Vishvaa: This Kala signifies the all-pervading, universal aspect of the sun. Vishvaa represents the sun's omnipresent nature, touching all aspects of life.

10. Vodhini: Associated with enlightenment or awakening, Vodhini symbolizes the enlightenment and awakening power of the sun, both literally and metaphorically.

11. Dhaarini: Meaning holding or supporting, Dhaarini represents the sustaining energy of the sun, its role in maintaining life and balance in the ecosystem.

12. Kshamaa: This Kala signifies patience or forgiveness, perhaps indicative of the sun's enduring, constant presence that overlooks all.

While these twelve names capture significant aspects of the sun's influence, traditionally, there are four more Kalas to make up the sixteen. These additional Kalas further elaborate on the diverse influences and qualities of the sun in Hindu and Tantric cosmology.

### *The four additional Kalas are -*

13. Prabha: This Kala signifies the radiance or the brilliant light of the sun, symbolizing clarity and the dispelling of darkness.

14. Nandini: Representing joy or delight, Nandini is the Kala that embodies the life-giving and nurturing aspect of the sun that brings happiness and vitality.

15. Suprabha: Meaning very bright or extremely luminous, Suprabha stands for the intense and magnificent brilliance of the sun.

16. Kaanti: This Kala signifies beauty or splendor, representing the aesthetic and inspiring aspect of sunlight that evokes beauty in nature.

In Tantric practices, the Chandra Kalas and Surya Kalas are not just seen as physical phases of the moon and sun but as spiritual energies that influence human life and consciousness. Their study and meditation are often part of advanced yogic and Tantric practices, where each Kala is understood to impart specific spiritual qualities and insights to the practitioner.

These Kalas are often studied and contemplated in advanced spiritual practices, particularly within certain schools of Tantra and yoga, where they are understood to be more than just physical phenomena. They are considered manifestations of subtle energies that have profound effects on the human body, mind, and spirit.

Chapter : 15

# The Dance of Karma: Destiny, Time, and the Spiritual Path

### *Understanding Karma*

In the intricate tapestry of life, the concept of Karma plays a pivotal role in shaping our spiritual journey. Derived from the Sanskrit word 'Kri', meaning 'to do', Karma is essentially the law of cause and effect. It posits that every action, thought, and emotion has a corresponding reaction, shaping our present and future. Why do some seem predestined for the spiritual path, while others embark on this journey later in life, and how taking even the smallest steps can lead us closer to the cosmic forces?

For some individuals, the call to spirituality seems ingrained, almost as if they were destined to walk this path. This sense of destiny could be a reflection of their Karma – the result of actions, learnings, and experiences accumulated over lifetimes. These souls are often quick to recognize and embrace their spiritual calling, as if resuming a journey paused in another time and place.

Conversely, many embark on their spiritual journey later in life or progress at a seemingly slower pace. This is not a reflection of their capabilities or potential but rather the rhythm of their own unique journey. Karma suggests that their experiences, lessons, and actions were necessary to reach the point where they can open themselves to spirituality. For these individuals, the path unfolds gradually, with each step being an integral part of their awakening.

While Karma implies predestination, it's important to recognize the role of free will. Our choices and actions in the present moment can alter the course of our journey, shaping our Karma. Thus, even those who may not feel an immediate connection to the spiritual path have the power to change their trajectory through conscious choices and actions.

For those still finding their way, the journey to spirituality does not require monumental leaps. Small, consistent steps can significantly impact one's spiritual development. Engaging in mindfulness, meditation, acts of kindness, and seeking knowledge can gradually clear the veil of ignorance, bringing us closer to the universal forces.

The spiritual path is inclusive and accessible to all, irrespective of where one stands in their journey. It's a path of compassion, understanding, and patience. Whether one is taking baby steps or strides, each movement towards spirituality is valuable and meaningful.

Each individual's journey is unique and should be embraced at its own pace. The journey to enlightenment is not a race; it's a deeply personal voyage of discovery, understanding, and connection with the universe. Comparing one's journey with others can be misleading and counterproductive.

In the grand scheme of existence, we are all part of this magnificent cosmic dance of Karma. Whether destined from the start or gradually awakening to the call, each soul has its place and time in the realm of spirituality. The key is to be open, to take those steps, however small they may seem, and trust in the journey. The forces of the universe work in tandem with our Karma, guiding us towards eventual awakening and enlightenment. Remember, every step towards spiritual growth, no matter how insignificant it may seem, brings us closer to being a part of the cosmic whole.

\*\*\*

The Shakti Peethas are significant shrines and pilgrimage destinations in Shaktism, the goddess-focused Hindu tradition. They are scattered across the Indian subcontinent. This list is according to the most common belief and folklore regarding the locations where parts of Sati's body are said to have fallen:

1. Hinglaj Mata Temple, Balochistan (Pakistan): It's believed that Sati's head fell here.
2. Kamakhya Temple, Assam: The site where Sati's womb and vagina fell.
3. Kali Ghat Temple, West Bengal: Sati's right toe is said to have fallen here.
4. Jwalamukhi Temple, Himachal Pradesh: The site where Sati's tongue fell.
5. Vishalakshi Temple, Varanasi, Uttar Pradesh: Sati's earrings are believed to have fallen here.
6. Naina Devi Temple, Himachal Pradesh: The site where Sati's eyes fell.
7. Mangla Gauri Temple, Bihar: Believed to be the location where Sati's breast fell.

8. Kalighat Temple, West Bengal: The site where Sati's right toes fell.
9. Ambaji Temple, Gujarat: It's said that Sati's heart fell here.
10. Shri Shail Temple, Bangladesh: The site where Sati's neck fell.
11. Mahalakshmi Temple, Kolhapur, Maharashtra: Sati's eyes are believed to have fallen here.
12. Ekaveerika Mata Temple, Maharashtra: The location where Sati's arm is said to have fallen.
13. Mahakali Temple, Ujjain, Madhya Pradesh: Believed to be where Sati's upper lip fell.
14. Puruhutika Temple, Andhra Pradesh: The site where Sati's left hand is said to have fallen.
15. Kanchi Kamakshi Temple, Tamil Nadu: Sati's navel is believed to have fallen here.
16. Sugandha Shakti Peeth, Bangladesh: The location where Sati's nose fell.
17. Biraja Temple, Odisha: Sati's navel is said to have fallen here.
18. Bahula Temple, West Bengal: This is the site where Sati's left arm fell.
19. Jayanti Shakti Peeth, Bangladesh: Where Sati's left thigh is believed to have fallen.
20. Kanyashram, Kerala: The location where Sati's back fell.
21. Bhramari Shakti Peeth, West Bengal: The site where Sati's left leg fell.

22. Chandranath Temple, Bangladesh: Believed to be the location where Sati's right arm fell.
23. Tripura Sundari Temple, Tripura: The site where Sati's right foot fell.
24. Trisrota Shakti Peeth, West Bengal: The location where Sati's left ankle fell.
25. Kireet Shakti Peeth, West Bengal: Where Sati's crown is said to have fallen.
26. Yogadya Shakti Peeth, West Bengal: The site where Sati's great toe fell.
27. Bhavani Shakti Peeth, Maharashtra: The location where Sati's head ornament fell.
28. Shakambhari Temple, Uttar Pradesh: The site where Sati's fingers fell.
29. Devi Patan Temple, Uttar Pradesh: It is believed that Sati's right shoulder fell here.
30. Vibhash, West Bengal: The site where Sati's left ankle fell.
31. Prabhas, Gujarat: Sati's stomach is said to have fallen here.
32. Bhadrakali Shakti Peeth, West Bengal: Believed to be where Sati's eyebrows fell.
33. Kalmadhav Shakti Peeth, Madhya Pradesh: The site where Sati's left buttock fell.
34. Shondesh, Bangladesh: The right buttock of Sati is believed to have fallen here.
35. Shri Parvat, Andhra Pradesh/Telangana border: This is the location where Sati's right anklet fell.

36. Kurukshetra, Haryana: The ankle bone of Sati is said to have fallen here.
37. Manivedika, Rajasthan: The right wrist of Sati is believed to have fallen here.
38. Ratnavali, West Bengal: The site where Sati's right shoulder fell.
39. Mithila, Bihar: The left shoulder of Sati is said to have fallen here.
40. Nandipur, Odisha: The necklace of Sati is believed to have fallen here.
41. Panchsagar, Uttar Pradesh: The lower teeth of Sati are said to have fallen here.
42. Loknath, Bangladesh: The location where Sati's throat fell.
43. Attahas, West Bengal: Sati's lips are believed to have fallen here.
44. Bakreshwar, West Bengal: The site where Sati's portion of the head or brain fell.
45. Jessoreswari, Bangladesh: The palatial region of Sati is said to have fallen here.
46. Prayaga, Uttar Pradesh: The fingers of Sati's left hand are believed to have fallen here.
47. Vrindavan, Uttar Pradesh: The ringlets of Sati's hair are said to have fallen here.
48. Shuchi, Bangladesh: The teeth of Sati are believed to have fallen here.
49. Ramgiri, Chhattisgarh: Believed to be the site where Sati's right breast fell.

50. Vartali, Gujarat: The site where Sati's upper lips are said to have fallen.
51. Ambika Shakti Peeth, Gujarat: Sati's heart is believed to have fallen here.
52. Shuchi Shakti Peeth, Tamil Nadu: The site where Sati's teeth fell.
53. Kottiyoor, Kerala: The location where Sati's naval fell.
54. Indrakshi Shakti Peeth, Tamil Nadu: Believed to be the site where Sati's right wrist fell.

The number of Shakti Peethas and their locations can vary significantly across different texts and regional traditions. Some texts mention 51, 52, or even more Shakti Peethas, and each has its own local myths and historical significance.

# Gratitude

*A Heartfelt Note of Gratitude*
*Dear Seekers of the Spiritual Path,*

*As I pen down these words, my heart is brimming with profound gratitude and a sense of deep connection with each one of you. You have not just been readers of this book; you have been fellow travellers on a journey that transcends the mere pages of text. It is with immense thankfulness that I acknowledge your presence in this shared exploration of the ancient ways of life and the mystical path of Tantra.*

*This book was not just a compilation of knowledge and experiences; it was a living tapestry woven with threads of curiosity, wisdom, and spiritual seeking. Each chapter we navigated together was more than just a topic; it was a stepping stone on our collective quest for understanding the profound aspects of existence. Your engagement, your thoughts, and your willingness to delve deep into the realm of the divine feminine with me have been invaluable.*

*In sharing this journey, we have created a bond, one that is anchored in the pursuit of higher knowledge and self-discovery. Through the pages of this book, we have traversed paths less travelled, unravelling mysteries, and unearthing truths that have been shrouded in the mists of time. Your companionship on this journey has been a source of encouragement and inspiration, reminding me that the quest for understanding the divine is a shared human endeavour.*

*As this chapter of our journey concludes, I want to assure you that this is merely a pause, not the end. My commitment to exploring and sharing the ancient ways of life, the profound teachings of Tantra, and the myriad paths of spiritual wisdom remains unwavering. I am already envisioning our next adventure together, delving deeper into the mystical and the sacred, uncovering truths, and experiencing the transformative power of ancient wisdom.*

*The path ahead is rich with possibilities and unexplored territories. I am excited about the prospect of bringing to you more teachings, more insights, and more revelations from the vast expanse of spiritual wisdom that our ancestors have left for us. The ancient ways are not just relics of the past; they are living, breathing wisdom that can guide us even in the modern world.*

*As we part ways, momentarily, from this shared journey, I urge you to carry the essence of what we have explored together in your hearts and minds. Let the essence of Kali and Her Yoginis, the insights into Tantra, and the revelations of the divine feminine continue to inspire and guide you in your personal quests.*

*Thank you, from the bottom of my heart, for being a part of this journey. Your presence has made this journey not just a solitary quest but a shared pilgrimage towards enlightenment. I eagerly anticipate our next meeting in the pages of another journey, another exploration into the mystical and the profound.*

*Until then, may your path be illuminated with wisdom, and may the divine feminine in all her forms continue to bless your journey with insight, strength, and peace.*

*With heartfelt gratitude and warm regards,*
*Meenakshii*
*Har Har Mahadev*

# Acknowledgements: Temples of Transformation

As I reflect upon the journey that has shaped the person I am today, my heart overflows with gratitude for the sacred sanctuaries that have been pivotal in my spiritual growth. These are not just places; they are vibrant abodes of divine energy, each holding a special place in the unfolding story of my life.

***Tara of Tarapeeth, West Bengal:*** Here, in the embrace of Tara Ma, I found resilience and the strength to face life's challenges. The profound spiritual energy of Tarapeeth has been a source of unending inspiration and solace.

***Kali of Kalighat, West Bengal:*** In the presence of Maa Kali at Kalighat, I experienced a transformative awakening. Her fierce compassion and protective embrace have guided me through life's darkest moments.

***Kashi Vishwanath, Uttar Pradesh:*** The sacred grounds of Kashi Vishwanath have been a haven of peace and spiritual renewal. Here, I connected with the timeless essence of faith and devotion.

***Puri Jagannath Temple, Puri:*** In the divine aura of Lord Jagannath, I found the embodiment of universal love and acceptance. This temple has been a guiding light in my journey of self-discovery.

***Bimala Temple, Puri, Orissa:*** The sanctuary of Goddess Bimala has been a source of divine feminine energy, empowering me to embrace my inner strength and wisdom.

***64 Yogini Peeth, Hirapur, Orissa:*** The mystical circle of the 64 Yoginis at Hirapur has been a profound source of learning about the divine feminine, enriching my soul with its ancient wisdom.

***64 Yogini Peeth of Madhya Pradesh:*** This sacred site has been instrumental in deepening my understanding of the cosmic play of energies and the intricate dance of the divine feminine.

***Kamakhya of Kamakhya Temple, Assam:*** The powerful Shakti of Goddess Kamakhya has been a transformative force, guiding me towards spiritual awakening and embracing the mysteries of life. By far, the most powerful of temples.

As I pen this note of deep gratitude, my thoughts turn reverently to a sacred space that has been instrumental in my spiritual journey - the ***Shiv-Kali-Manasa Temple***, a divine sanctuary lovingly built by my late grandparents, Sri Bijoy Ranjan Das and Smt. Sovana Das. This hallowed ground, more than just a structure of worship, has been a guiding star in my quest for spiritual understanding and growth.

***A Legacy of Devotion:*** The temple, envisioned and created by my revered grandparents, stands as a testament to their devotion and spiritual foresight. It has been a constant source of inspiration, reminding me of the profound legacy of faith and dedication they have bequeathed.

***Two Decades of Havan(fire) Rituals:*** For over twenty years, every Amavasya has seen me partake in the sacred fire rituals within the temple's sanctified walls. This unbroken chain of devotion observed no matter the circumstances, has been a cornerstone of my spiritual practice.

In moments of doubt and uncertainty, the temple has been my sanctuary, a place where clarity and solace were always within reach. Its sacred flames have not only consumed the physical offerings but also illuminated the darker corners of my soul, guiding me towards inner peace and understanding.

This temple has been much more than a place of worship; it has been a teacher, a companion, and a portal to the divine. The lessons learned and the insights gained within its embrace have been pivotal in shaping my spiritual path.

*The Shiv-Kali-Manasa Temple*, a cherished creation of my grandparents, will always hold a special place in my heart. I am eternally grateful for this sacred and powerful space that has shown me the path, nurtured my faith, and provided a steadfast anchor in my spiritual voyage. May the legacy of this temple continue to inspire and guide not only me but also future generations in their pursuit of spiritual fulfilment.

*Ashoknagar, Maniktala, North 24 Parganas, West Bengal.*

Each of the above-mentioned sacred places has bestowed upon me invaluable lessons, blessings, and experiences, shaping my spiritual path and growth. I extend my deepest gratitude to these divine sanctuaries for being the pillars of light and wisdom in my life's journey. May the blessings of these holy sites continue to guide and nurture all who seek spiritual enlightenment.

With heartfelt reverence and eternal gratitude..

www.ingramcontent.com/pod-product-compliance
Lightning Source LLC
LaVergne TN
LVHW061542070526
838199LV00077B/6867